Acclaim for Elliot Rais'
Stealing the Borders

"It's one of the best books I've read this year, amusing, witty and down to earth. Great cinematic appeal. Hollywood should grab it fast."

— Ivor Davis / New York Times Syndicate

"It made me cry. It made me laugh. It was so good, I can't believe I didn't write it myself."

— Jackie Mason

"...Fascinating. It's hard to put it down."

— Madeline Kahn

"...absorbing, amusing, and philosophically worthwhile reading ... a rare talent ... Throw yourself into this fascinating life history..."

— Albert Ellis, Ph.D.
Author, New Guide To Rational Living

"Warm, witty...Worth the read ... THUMBS UP."

— Indianapolis News

"Stealing The Borders: A Warm, Witty and Outrageous Autobiography ... absurd and humor filled story..."

— MENSA Bulletin
The Magazine of American Mensa

"Stealing The Borders will steal your heart."

— The Ridgewood News

"The guy is hilarious, and has a keenly developed sense of the absurd."

— Santa Fe Sun

"...a gentle mix of Mordechai Richler's The Apprenticesbip of Duddy Kravitz and Elia Kazan's America America. A wonderful read. A movie waiting to happen."

—Ken Dancyger
Author, Alternative Script Writing

"...the literary ingredients that make for 'Best Seller'... adaptation to TV or the silver screen seems a natural."

— George Bernard
Author, Inside The National Enquirerv

Stealing the Borders

by Elliot Rais

Originally published in the US as a paperback in 1994

For information contact Elliot Rais
StealingTheBorders@gmail.com

Copyright © Elliot Rais 1994, 2012

ISBN-10: 1467901571
ISBN-13: 9781467901574

Dedicated to

MICHAEL and LAUREN, that they may better understand the forces that molded their father and thus their own lives.

MY SISTER, whom I love even if she did snatch some insects from my hungry jaws.

MY FATHER, who threw me onto the train, so that I could live to write about it.

MY MOTHER, whose nurturing got me through the remaining journey.

Note:

For simplicity, the writer often makes references to Russia, when in reality it is the Ukraine, Azerbaijan, or other parts or the Soviet Union.

Doctor
(9:00 A.M. July 2, 1982 age 42)

Please, doctor, give me a pen and paper. Maybe I can distract myself by writing something. Perhaps I'll write a poem about the surgery you're performing on me. I can't stand to hear the sound of your scissors snipping at my skin. - Thank you very much.

Here I lie
  with butt midair
Trying to
  act debonair.

Perhaps a joke
  I'll try to be cute
Break the doctor's
  serious mood.

I hear him laugh
    oh, what a break
But not too much
    his hand may shake

And miss the mark
    by inches few
Thereby create
    a person new

With gender of
    a different kind
A wiggling butt -
    an altered mind.

God, didn't they snip off enough when they circumcised me? Do they want to take off the rest? What is it, am I being punished for getting divorced? Wait a minute, let's not get crazy, they're not taking anything off me. They're just removing a little growth, and it's on my leg, and it's at least three inches away from my privates.

I've got to stop acting like a child. I'm forty-two years old and behaving like a child. Who looks worried - me? Of course me! It can't be the doctor.

He's holding the scalpel. Maybe I should hold the scalpel and then the doctor could look worried.

"The problem is, doctor, I didn't choose a good day for an operation!"

"Elliot, is there such a day?"

"Well maybe not, but there are probably better days. Take the waiting room, for instance."

"You don't like the waiting room at New York University Medical Center?"

"No, that's not it. While in the waiting room I was reading today's New York Times. It seems that the paper that prints all the news that's fit to print also knows the most fitting time to print it. Staring at me on page A 23 is an article titled 'How to Ease the Pain.' Jumping out of the page especially to greet me is a sentence that states, 'The modern physician is regarded as a competent technician who is cold, aloof, mercenary...' Are you a 'modern physician'? Let me get to the point, are you mercenary? Do I really need this procedure? Sorry, doctor, I didn't mean that - of course I need it (I think). Ooooh - I know, doctor, this won't hurt a bit. That's what they also told me when I was seven years old and got circumcised. And that was followed by four weeks of memorable pain!"

"Why did they circumcise you at the age of seven?"

"Because I was stupid enough to let them, that's why!"

"How so?"

"Well, it's a long story, and I hope I don't stay on this surgical table that long. Besides, I'm too worried to talk."

"Stop worrying. We already told you it's benign, it's just a little growth you can do without. Now, why were you circumcised at the age of seven?"

"You don't want to hear that whole story."

"Sure we do. We get bored doing surgery and might otherwise fall asleep in the middle."

"I'll tell! I'll tell!"

Circumcision
(1947 - age 7)

Our dwelling was part of a long row of attached gray townhouses, each looking exactly like the next. When we had first arrived there two years earlier, I was afraid to leave the house for fear I would not find it again. My parents tied a small string to the front door to help me identify it. I feared that the string could disappear and that I would be lost forever. At the age of five I did not understand that I was not going to wander off too far, not for the next seven years. Our new home was in the middle of a DP (displaced persons) camp in Germany.

But now it was 1947, two years after the war had ended. I was seven years old and quite accustomed to this life. My father gripped my small hand firmly and tugged lovingly as he announced that we were going to the public bath. Has it been a whole week already? I still feel so clean. Here, Dad, smell me! Look, don't I look clean!

Although bathing was a nuisance, I didn't really mind it that much. After all, it meant I was going to march proudly down the whole length of the camp toward the communal shower, holding hands with my father. Having witnessed his near demise a few years earlier, I was appreciative of having a father at all, but I felt particularly lucky to have this man as my father. In this camp of war survivors, he looked as if he had entered on some special pass. The other men in camp appeared war beaten and worn down by the Holocaust. Not so with my father. He spoke in a jovial and assured manner, always coming up with something bright or witty to say. My father radiated an assurance as though he had a master plan, or as if he knew something, his etched smile lines belying the horrors his deep-set eyes had witnessed.

I thought everybody admired and was attracted to my father. I was his son, and so proud to walk hand in hand down the camp with him. "Hey, everyone see us together. Yes, this is my father!" In contrast, I was a scrawny little kid. But behold my father! I'm going to look and be like him someday.

The communal baths were taken for ritualistic as well as for sanitary reasons. Although I had been in these communal baths many times before, this time was different. This time I suddenly became aware of something. You see, at the age of seven, I was at a perfect height to observe the other men's genitals. I suddenly became aware that I was distinctly different. I pointed out to my father that although he had a fine specimen, in keeping with the style of the place, mine was definitely different. This was very upsetting to me. "Why am I different?" I implored. He insisted that we not discuss it until we returned home.

When we arrived home, I could see my mother's back as she tasted the soup she was preparing. The kitchen was rich with fragrance; it smelled good; it was her special chicken soup. As she lifted the spoon to taste, I could see her golden teeth glisten through the clear soup.

My mother, a short bosomy woman with straight hair and a smooth complexion, was decidedly overweight, although you could not call her obese. Her plump stature was somewhat of an embarrassment to me. We had all lived through the war in semi-starvation. Everyone was skinny. It was the fashion. How could she be fat? Was she sneaking? Hoarding food? I knew that couldn't be so. After all, my mother would have torn off her own flesh to feed me. How could I even think that she was hoarding food? Then again, why was she fat?

Although she was bright and a touch more progressive than the other women in the camp, in Father's presence her position was clear. If we walked somewhere, my father always walked two steps ahead of her. He was careful to keep that arrangement; she allowed it. My feet moved quickly, to keep up with my father.

Once again I began to press for an explanation regarding the differences I had noticed at the public bath. My parents had some discomfort discussing this issue, but finally responded that the other men were all circumcised because they were Jewish.

Hey, what's the story here, I said, I'm Jewish, too. Am I not a good Jew? Why am I not circumcised? What an indignity! How was I ever to take a communal bath again with all the Jewish men waving their fine badges of belonging? It was plain to see that mine was different. But I wanted to belong, too.

My parents explained that the difference stemmed from the fact that I wasn't circumcised.

They told me that all Jews get circumcised and that the circumcision was usually performed in the first week after birth. They explained that I was born in the midst of the war, during a time when everyone was preoccupied with survival. Under those circumstances, there was no possibility of having a circumcision party.

I missed my circumcision party? Wait a minute, did I hear party? Now we're talking cake and maybe even a present as well as becoming a real Jew. "I want that party!"

I didn't make much headway with my parents, although they were mumbling something to each other about an omen. They had been content to forgo the circumcision, but perhaps this was an omen. God could be instructing them through my lips to fulfill their Jewish obligation. My grandfather, a self-professed authority on such matters, assured them that this must be the case.

I lost patience with my parents and protested directly to the rabbi about how my parents wouldn't allow me to become a real Jew. Well, the rabbi wasted no time in gathering a pious posse and presenting himself at my parents' home. The rabbi, with the support of the posse, assured my parents that my request for the circumcision was definitely an omen. God was instructing me to join the fold, and my parents had better not interfere. He so much as guaranteed them that my request for the circumcision was an omen. He was sure of it. He was also armed with biblical quotations to support his case.

My parents, overwhelmed by the cumulative pressure of the rabbi, the posse and the quotations, finally yielded. The circumcision was agreed to and was scheduled.

My day! What a party! Everyone squeezed into my home. Friends, relatives, strangers, curiosity seekers, freeloaders. The food preparation had gone on for a whole week.

I was the celebrity. Even without the benefit of a PR man or a press release, people from all around knew about this seven-year-old and the omen.

Everything was fine until the mohel arrived. I didn't know about this character, with a beard and sideburns hanging to his chest. I could only see his eyes and red lips peeking through the hair. He wore a special robe and commanded the crowd's attention, so I sensed that he was important and had something to do with the ritual. The party continued as before.

A few minutes after his appearance, the mohel invited me over to a corner and asked me to lower my trousers. At that age, this presented no special difficulty for me. I would offer my penis for inspection to anyone. After examining it, he unrolled a cloth that contained knives and other sharp-looking apparatus. He examined each knife in succession, intermittently checking my genitals, as if to determine which tool was the sharpest and best suited for this particular job. You can't have a circumcision without a mohel. He is the one who knows what prayers to say, when to say them, and most important, what piece to cut off when he says them.

Suddenly it all came together. This circumcision business wasn't just eating cake, drinking wine, and making prayers. There could be a lot of pain that went along with this ritual. It was all coming back to me. I had attended numerous other circumcision parties. There was always lots of home baked cake, wine, praying, singing and joy. Then there was the part of the ceremony where someone held a baby. A person who looked very much like this mohel would huddle next to him. At that point, all of the grownups would crowd around the mohel and the infant. I was always too small to push my way up front and too short to see what was going on. Besides, there was so much cake and so little time. Always, someone would say a prayer in Hebrew, followed by tremendous shrieking from the infant. I never understood why.

Suddenly I had a flash of insight. The mohel, the knives, the infant shrieking. This was no party I wanted to be at. These barbarians were going to carve me up.

No, that's not possible. My father is here; he wouldn't let them do that to me. On the other hand, Grandpa had recently told me the biblical story of Abraham and Isaac. In it, God told Abraham he wanted a sacrifice. Not a chicken or a lamb, but Abraham's own son Isaac. Abraham was ready to oblige. Did God ask my father for a sacrifice? Is there anything else I wasn't told?

I took off. I ran with my life's breath. I managed to get out of the apartment and through the backyard. The rabbi and his posse closed in like a pack of wolves who had inhaled the first whiff of a rabbit's blood. Reality closed in. It was not my party, it was theirs, and they were determined not to let me spoil it.

They were gaining on me. The only way out of the garden was to leap over the rosebushes. I dove as hard as I could. Ouch, they caught me. The thorns and the zealots conspired to foil my escape.

Once back inside, they held me down and administered ether. The sedation was administered by the clergy instead of a physician. They were accustomed to dealing with newborns, where they used only a drop of wine for sedation. With me they used ether, but an inadequate amount. I slid in and out of various depths of consciousness, often feeling excruciating pain. During my restless "sleep" under sedation, I had kaleidoscopic visions of the mohel with his knives and a dozen or so of his clones. They were in a circle dancing around me with knives in their hands and songs coming out of their very red lips. The beards were long and knotted to each other. They were eating, singing and cutting me up, each activity seemingly giving them equal pleasure.

I was the one who had asked for the circumcision. I was a child and I thought a circumcision was something given to you. I felt betrayed when I finally grasped that a circumcision wasn't something you're given, but something that's taken. Why didn't anyone explain that to me? Why didn't anyone explain to me how painful this was going to be?

"Unlike this surgery, doctor, my circumcision was entered into without informed consent."

"Sounds dreadful, Elliot, to be betrayed at such a young age."

"On the contrary, doctor. Here I was only seven years old, and I had already had the advantage of understanding the true nature of humanity."

"And what may that be, Elliot?"

"Putting it crudely, the lesson I learned was that if you let him, your fellowman will cut off your balls. Furthermore, even the people who love you most, like your parents, can be duped into acquiescence in the name of religion, or patriotism or something."

"Has this experience made you bitter?"

"No, the experience equipped me very well for life. I learned to observe and ask many questions before I leap, and more importantly, I learned that if others want to cut off part of their penises, it doesn't mean that I have to do the same. So you see, doctor, this painful experience had its own reward built in. I enjoy life more because I learned to see the humor, or madness, in it and to protect my balls at all times. Which reminds me, be careful, doctor, watch what you're doing!"

"So the circumcision was postponed until you were seven years old because you were born in Poland?"

"No, not necessarily."

"Not because you were born in Poland?"

"No! It's just that I wasn't necessarily born in Poland."

"How can you be uncertain about where you were born?"

"There are some things I'm uncertain of. That's the kind of life I've had."

"What kind of life was that?"

EASTERN EUROPE :
Life in Poland
(1940 - age 0)

L ate in 1939, as Hitler advanced into Poland, my father decided it was time to leave. This was a difficult decision because for most of his life the family had been struggling. It was only in the half dozen or so years prior to the war that my father had developed a measure of prosperity, and he was reluctant to part with it.

My father owned a mill, where local peasantry brought their grain to be ground into flour. However, since in Poland Jews were not allowed to own land in their own name, my father had a deal with a Polish noblewoman, in whose name everything was held. Since virtually everything he owned was tied to the land, leaving Poland also meant leaving penniless.

There were four of us in my family. Well, almost. There was my father, my mother, my six-year-old sister, and me. Well, there wasn't a "me" yet, but my mother was already pregnant as final preparations were being made to flee from Hitler and Poland by moving east into Russia.

Many people were leaving Poland, but many others, who refused to believe the rumors of the impending atrocities, refused to leave and remained in Poland. When my father announced he was leaving Poland, everyone on his side of the family except his brother decided to follow. This included my father's parents and his five younger, still unmarried, sisters. Nobody on my mother's side joined the exodus. The members of our family that remained in Poland perished under Hitler. The ones that left Poland survived.

The family lived in a part of Poland that was near Russia. The exit from Poland to Russia was by foot. With border changes and the general prevailing confusion of war, it's not totally clear to me where I was born. Some family members place my birth in Poland, others in Russia. The only thing they all agree on is that it was in a forest. The family members that credited Poland as my birthplace referred to me by the name of "Siroza." The ones who delighted in thinking of me as a Russian called me "Sasha." They all concurred that my Hebrew name would be "Israel," and thus it followed that in Yiddish (the preferred language), I would be called "Srulic." The end result was that as far back as I can recall, if anyone called out any name at all, I would answer first and analyze after whether that was one of the names assigned to me. If a boy named Sue becomes tough, a boy with four names at birth becomes flexible and accommodating, if somewhat perplexed.

Anyway, if you ask me whether my family really doesn't know where I was born, I couldn't tell you for sure, but I can tell you that they certainly haven't taken heroic measures to clarify it for me.

Enter Russia
(Age 1 to 5)

Russia needed workers in its far northern regions. The forests needed to be logged. There were posters at the borders promising the immigrants plentiful work in the north. We went there, far north and west of Siberia, to the part of Russia that almost touches Finland.

The weather was subhuman. My mother and I, just newly born, almost died. We lived in a little outpost deep in the forest. No hospitals nor civilization nearby. Food was nearly nonexistent. What little food there was in Russia was being grown much further south. Russia's distribution system was totally inadequate for getting any of the food up north.

The hopelessness of the situation was clear to all. It was clear that death by cold or starvation were imminent. We were desperate to leave. My father heard that conditions were better down south. Through great manipulation and contrivance, he found a way to persuade the authorities to allow us to migrate south. In Russia, without proper papers one couldn't travel, much less relocate. We wound up near the Black Sea for a while, but as Germany advanced bombs were falling all around us. One exploded and shattered the window over my crib. My parents dusted the glass off me and moved further east.

This is where I spent most of my first five years. I don't know how much of those five years I really remember. I've heard the story of this part of my life from relatives so many times that I cannot differentiate between my own memory and their collective memory. These were hard times of bare survival, and I know I remember at least the latter part of that experience.

We settled in a town called Agdam, in the southwestern part of the Soviet Union, just west of the Caspian Sea, near the Iranian border. Having arrived in Russia at a time when Russia was at war and could barely manage to feed her soldiers, we could not expect to be cared for by an intricate bureaucracy that could barely care for those who knew the ropes.

Compounding our problems, my father was drafted into the Soviet Army shortly after our arrival. The

Russian method of conscription seemed to defy their own complex bureaucracy. In fact, it was admirably efficient and highly effective. They hardly had to draft at all. They simply posted signs announcing that all able-bodied men between certain ages who do not enlist are considered traitors. Everyone knew that traitors are put against a wall and executed. The prevailing fear and panic caused able-bodied men to virtually leap onto passing military trucks.

Arrests among immigrants were not rare. As there was inadequate food, those who had any entrepreneurial ability would try to hustle. For instance, a woman could knit a sweater, trade it to a soldier for cigarettes, trade the cigarettes to a butcher for some meat, trade some of the meat for more wool, and have some meat left over to feed the family. All in all, not a huge business, it was nevertheless highly punishable, since conducting any business in Russia was illegal. Those who also had some cigarettes for the policemen fared considerably better.

During this time in Russia we lived in a little house/shack. The total size of the house was approximately nine feet by twelve feet. In this one room lived my grandparents, my parents, my sister, myself and my father's five sisters, one of whom, by now, had a husband. The house consisted of four walls, a window and a door, no kitchen or bath, and a dirt floor, with some kind of rug over it. My mother hung a curtain on the window and it was home. That was my first reality. I didn't feel crowded at all.

While my father was in the Army, my mother was usually out somewhere trying to obtain food. Agdam is in tropical Russia, so heating wasn't necessary. Cooking, when there was something to cook, occurred outdoors. There was a pit in the ground with metal walls, kind of like a submerged trash can. A fire would be lit in the bottom of it, and dough would be flattened out and slapped against its walls. There the dough would bake until removed. Kind of like well-done pizza (hold the cheese, tomatoes and anchovies), but no one complained.

Much of the time most of the people were out of the house, attending to the task of earning, trading or finding food. My sister, six years older than I, attended the public school all day. She received a decent education and learned to read and write Russian. She was the nearest thing to a peer that I had, but was preoccupied with school and her own life. I always wanted to go where she went, but of course I wasn't allowed to. I felt that she received much more attention than I did, and I was jealous.

I don't recall feeling lonesome, however, as there was always a great deal of activity, people coming and going in and out of the house. Anyone passing by was for the moment like a parent to me. My parents and my other relatives were interchangeable. One of my aunts had had a child one year younger than I was. When her child died, she shared in breastfeeding me. Not much effort was spent to engage me in conversation as there were more life-threatening matters to attend to. It was also generally accepted that I was incapable of speaking.

Russian Bazaar
(1943 - age 3)

By the time I was two years old, I was generally put outdoors for the day. At the end of the day I would be fetched in. We lived adjacent to an outdoor flea market where merchants displayed their wares on a sheet or carpet laid on the ground. It was typical of what you would picture as a market in Turkey, Afghanistan or Iran, the bordering countries in the region. I was a permanent fixture among the merchants, and someone would always know where to find me. I loved the outdoor market and could always entertain myself there. It was a bustling place. Everything imaginable could be bought, sold, or traded there. I meandered from vendor to vendor, socializing with them. During their slow hours they found me a source of entertainment. As I was hungry most of the time, I pursued anything that crawled and put it in my mouth. If I could catch something, I'd eat it. Sometimes all my stalking was in vain, for as soon as I put my trophy in my mouth, some adult would retrieve it and deprive me of it.

Some food was sold in the market. Potential buyers were permitted to put their fingers in the thick sour cream to taste it before purchasing. From time to time, I emulated the potential purchasers, putting my fingers in the cream, licking them, and exclaiming some appropriate remarks that I had learned to imitate. This met with various degrees of success, depending on how amusing I proved to the vendors.

My family was concerned about me. Even though my physical development was normal, I still was not talking. If I wanted something, I just grunted and pointed to it. One day, at the age of three or so, I really wanted something. I wanted an item that resembled chewing gum, and I knew exactly which vendor had it. I grabbed my mother by the arm, pulled, motioned, grunted, and insisted that she come with me. I led her to the vendor and pointed to the object of my desire. When she produced the money to pay, however, I intervened, and commenced to negotiate as I had witnessed others do so many times. My mother was flabbergasted to discover that I spoke in Azerbaijani, the language spoken by local population in that region. What she had thought to be a disability turned out to be merely a lack of communication between me and the other members of my family. They were constantly coming and going, giving me affection, and food when available, whereas the locals in the marketplace used to speak to me. So, naturally, I had no use for Yiddish and a great deal of use for Azerbaijani. Following this discovery, I learned Yiddish as well.

Father Returns
(1944 - age 4)

Father finally returned from the army. Once he came home he started wheeling and dealing, and things got much better for us. I was privileged to have things like black bread with sour cream, and I stopped eating bugs. Well, I didn't stop eating bugs completely, not cold turkey, that is. I was still always a little hungry, and they did add a certain flavor to the sour cream.

Packages were always coming and leaving the house. People came and went. Food, cigarettes, leather, stuff of all kinds. Soldiers, cops, in and out. I saw all the activities.

In a government cleanup one day, some inspectors apparently were led to our home. They came in and announced a search. They searched everywhere, but found nothing (the search had been anticipated; our illegal goods had been camouflaged or disposed of). The officials, ready to leave, exclaimed loudly to my father, "We know you are engaging in enterprise and that you are hiding things from us!"

My father denied it. He said, "No, absolutely not!"

I, in my childish innocence, reminded my father that he indeed was hiding things, adding that it was not nice to lie. I led everyone to the goods.

My father was apprehended, placed against the wall, with drawn guns. I thought he was to be shot. I was in a corner screaming in terror. My father was going to be shot, and I knew I was to blame. What would I do without my father? He had finally come back from the war to be my father, to love me, to feed me, and I had done something to have him shot. No more father. My mother and my aunts would surely kill me for doing this terrible thing.

What had I done wrong to cause all this chaos? It was so puzzling. My father - he's the one who taught me to tell the truth. Was he himself lying when he told me that I must always tell the truth? I was too young to sort that out.

Finally, in tears, my mother threw herself on the mercy of the commander, promising favors and payoffs. A deal was struck, and my father was spared.

It is now 1945. I am five years old. As a result of the threatened execution, my father had cooled down his business activities considerably. The war was over, but the chaos, confusion, and hunger weren't. My father, in his forties, had too much entrepreneurial spirit to adapt to Communism. The family wanted out of Russia. But to leave the Soviet bloc proved most tedious. It was like a Roach Motel: You could check in, but you couldn't check out. My father decided that there was sufficient chaos immediately after the war to make a run to Western Europe. When my father, the family patriarch, decided it was time to leave, the whole family, including his parents and his sisters, followed, as they had followed him into Russia.

Exit Russia
(1945 - age 5)

The migration took months and covered thousands of miles. We trekked through Russia, Poland, Czechoslovakia and Austria before we finally wound up in Germany. I'm often asked why my father went to Germany, whether he was looking to jump out of the frying pan into the fire. But it was a good choice. Germany was occupied by the Allies, there were DP camps throughout Germany, and sanctuary could be found in these camps.

Although much of the journey was by freight train, I remember also having to walk a lot. Certain legs of the journey were particularly perilous and had to be planned carefully, such as the exit from Poland to Czechoslovakia. A caravan was formed, and a guide was hired. We had to walk through the wilderness for a few days and nights, with some intermediate stops.

In preparation for the long walk through the forest, we were constantly reminded how essential it was that we all remain absolutely silent, for the slightest noise could give our position away to the frontier guards, whereupon the whole caravan would be shot. I also kept hearing how we were going to lose the night "stealing the border" (a Yiddish idiom meaning escape). I protested vehemently and reminded everyone that it was forbidden to steal. Nevertheless, I understood the seriousness of remaining quiet, for I was already five years old and knew what had happened to my father when I said he was lying. I really knew the meaning of life and death very well. I didn't, however, understand how we would find the night that we had lost. Where did it go?

The forest was dark and frightening. Very few people in our group of approximately fifty had flashlights. One of my uncles, a tall, muscular carpenter, had a flashlight. I knew he was my best bet for survival, and I hung onto him dearly for much of that journey.

We finally arrived at what seemed like a clearing in the middle of the forest. There were only the tracks, a very long freight train, and a water tank that filled the locomotive with massive amounts of water.

Once more, we boarded the cattle cars. Each car had a floor, four walls, and four square portholes for air. Again, families staked out their areas with blankets. This was all very familiar, we had already been living on trains for weeks during this passage for freedom.

Periodically, the train stopped at some desolate place to fill up with water. If the stop was long enough, passengers disembarked to relieve themselves, wash up if possible, stretch their legs, and escape the stink and confinement of the cattle car, even if only for a moment.

At one particular stop I was challenged to a game of chicken by a boy who was somewhat older than I. We waited for the train whistle to blow, and as the last adult climbed aboard, we began to race towards the moving train. The train seemed to pull out with less lead time than we had experienced previously. The makeshift stepladder had already been pulled up, and my challenger's hand barely managed to reach the grip of an adult who pulled him up.

I was slightly behind him, and the gap was increasing as the train accelerated. All my shouts, and the shouts of the adults calling out to me, fell on deaf ears, as the conductor was way in front of our car.

I saw my life slipping away and was sure I would be devoured by bears or wolves as soon as the sun fell completely. At the last possible moment, my father became aware of the situation. He jumped off, managed to throw me on board, and barely managed to grab onto the accelerating train, pulling himself up with a great struggle. I can still see his feet dangling off the ground as he finally managed to pull himself onto the train floor.

It was a long time ago - I was only five years old - but the image of that freight car pulling out without me is engraved deeply in my mind. I remember the event as if it happened yesterday. Why did it take my father so long to realize my peril? What if he hadn't noticed the situation for another moment? I knew he loved me, as all my relatives did, as well as some of the other people on that train. So how come I almost perished?

Thinking back, I realize that that experience preceded the circumcision experience. The frailty of life was already being pointed out to me. Yes, I had already begun to understand how vulnerable we all are, and that I had better learn to take care of my own little ass, because others, even those who care, may not always be there to save me on time. The seeds of my self-reliance were sown by that event. It was a lesson I'm glad I learned, and yet still I wish I hadn't had to learn it at such a tender age.

The train finally brought us to Germany, where I spent the next seven years of my life.

Western Europe: DP Camp ~ Germany
(Age 5 to 11)

O nce we arrived at the DP camp in Germany, the first order of business was to settle into housing. Forms, papers, lines, inoculations. Then we were issued an apartment with a kitchen, a gas stove, and four bedrooms. Everyone got into the purifying acts of rubbing, scrubbing, fixing and painting. My mother hung curtains on the windows, and it became home.

The apartment accommodated our family luxuriously. My grandparents took one bedroom, my aunts took two, and my parents with my sister and myself had one bedroom all to ourselves. We all shared the one kitchen. It seemed like the height of luxury. It was a haven in heaven, in a country in hell.

Alive! Joy and relief was in the air. But grieving was there, too. Many people had lost their loved ones. My mother lost absolutely everyone on her side of the family; my father lost his brother. With the joy, there was also an undercurrent of guilt surrounding survival, almost like a sense of betrayal of all the loved ones that had perished. "How come I survived?" people asked themselves. "How dare I be happy about life, about surviving, when so many loved ones perished? How dare I ever be happy again at all?"

The possibility of a new life was, however, what dominated. Everyone was glad to have survived. Hope was everywhere. Hope of finding a war-scattered relative. Every day you heard in the street about someone who had taken his brother, or sister, mother, father, or uncle, for dead and discovered him or her alive and well in some other DP camp, or another country.

The DP camp was like a summer camp. Although there were thousands of people in each camp, everyone seemed to know everyone else. If one wasn't known by sight, then certainly by family, or by the village from where one originated. Yiddish was the primary language in camp, but every other European language could be heard. There was no employment in the camp, and certainly none to be had for Jews outside of the camp. Everyone had the same job: waiting to emigrate.

The men stood together on street corners and exchanged stories. One got a letter from America attesting that the streets were full of milk and honey. Another heard from a cousin in Peru that business opportunities there were great because labor was so inexpensive. Yet another held a newspaper clipping detailing how many people the U.S. would allow to immigrate that particular year, and how many more people were still in the DP camps. Excitement was also brewing in Palestine.

There was a lot of idleness among the men, and that sometimes led to mischief. Fistfights were rare, but sometimes cruelty unleashed itself in other ways. Every so often some adults (or what seemed to me like adults at the time) would tie two dogs' tails together and watch them brutally attack each other, each dog surmising that the other dog was somehow responsible for its own dilemma. I watched, but I was horrified. If the dogs' mothers and fathers were there, these men probably wouldn't get away with that, I thought.

I didn't like the cruelty, and didn't understand why these men did that.

Everything was temporary. A month, two months, soon we'd be in America, Bolivia, Peru, Palestine (which had now become Israel), or someplace else wonderful, with much opportunity and no persecution. The weeks turned into months. The months turned into years. The adults were getting restless. Some developed little enterprises to keep busy and to make some money.

Aware that people loitered all day in camp, my parents began whipping up ice cream in our kitchen and selling it on the corner. There were many corners, so the ice cream business grew. Soon my parents had a slew of sophisticated equipment in a large basement. Some of the previously unemployed could now work for my father selling ice cream in our camp, as well as in some of the other DP camps in Germany.

Life wasn't particularly bad for me. Everyone knew I was the boss's son. I could walk up to any corner and get ice cream. I was cavalier about it. I would bring my friends to a corner ice cream stand and we would all receive free ice cream. This gave me a sense of power with the other little kids. One day I went a little too far.

I left a window open in my father's factory and reentered later with a group of my friends for an impromptu feast. We left the place in shambles. My parents were very angry. I didn't see what the big deal was. I just wanted to have a party. I overheard my mother telling my grandmother that I had just done something childish, and that I would of course grow up. I saw no point in growing up so that I could do grownup things. I wasn't going to tie dogs' tails together to watch them cannibalize each other.

As a child, camp wasn't at all a bad place to be brought up. Sure, missing my education was a problem that I had to work very hard later in life to overcome. But in return, I gained a very unique perception of life and life's struggles. Children and adults lived together, confronted life and death together. There was no such thing as a babysitter.

For the adults, the years after the war spent in DP camps had to be more painful than the war itself. The war was full of survival activity, whereas camp was a fatal suspension, a total negation of life, as if to punish people who had survived a journey through the seven stages of hell just because they survived.

Growing
(Age 5 to 11)

If I found an old bicycle tire rim, I could play with it by striking it with a stick and causing it to roll. Two discarded tin cans connected with a string sufficed as a walkie-talkie. Imagination was always the key ingredient. Nothing I owned came packed with instructions on how to use it or enjoy it.

I owned only two purchased toys. My favorite one was the squeeze box. When you own only two toys, you learn to cherish them. They become your friends. You get to observe and know them very well. You learn from them. There are of course other advantages of owning only two toys. You always know where your toys are, you have no trouble finding your favorite toy, and if your mother ever does yell at you to put away all your toys, it's a cinch.

Even though purchased toys were rare, my friends and I had no lack of activity. I never heard the expression "Mommy, I'm bored" until I came to the U.S. Daily activities accounted for much of our amusement.

We had chickens in the backyard. We weren't raising them, but since there were no refrigerators we had to buy a few at a time and keep them alive until we were ready to eat them. When the occasion called for chicken, I would catch the unfortunate fowl, tie its legs together, slide the handlebars of my bicycle through its legs, and ride to the center of the DP camp. The bird, upside down, would flap its wings frantically during the journey to the shoichet.

For a bird to be deemed kosher, it must be slaughtered by a shoichet. A shoichet is a specialist who can say the proper prayer and slash the bird's throat in a way that I was told is painless to the bird. Much the way a mohel makes a prayer and cuts the penis, the shoichet makes a prayer and cuts the throat. It seems a common principal in many religions that it's okay to cut anything as long as you know the right prayer to say.

I always watched the procedure, but I could not be convinced that this was a big thrill for the bird.

I didn't see this as much different from tying two dogs together and watching them kill each other, except that the dogs had a greater opportunity to escape with their lives. The poor chicken was scared, helpless and hopeless. Unless it was fluent in Yiddish, and very persuasive with the shoichet, there was no way that that chicken would leave the premises alive.

Once executed, the bird was again mounted on the bike for its return home, with droplets of blood marking the path. I did what I was supposed to, but I hated it. The bird was as likely as not to have been my pet preceding its demise. I didn't want to eat the chicken even though it tasted better than the bugs. At least the bugs weren't my pets. Yes, I remained a skinny kid for quite some time.

Like children everywhere, we played games. Our version of Cowboys and Indians was "Kill the Nazis." It was easy to simulate a war theater, as there were still piles of rubble here and there, and there were fences of every description in and around this DP camp. Germany excelled in building fences. Who could resist climbing, mastering and defying these fences? Hiding and trying not to be shot as we were stealing some imaginary border, we all knew something about that.

This was a child's paradise. Sometimes the MPs (military police) would come to the camp. It was a joy for the kids to hear their arrival, announced by the dogs chasing their jeeps. Motor vehicles were extremely rare in camp and drove the dogs berserk.

When the MPs left their jeeps, the kids jumped aboard. We enjoyed simulating driving. On one occasion I managed to move enough buttons and gears to actually start the jeep, loaded with a bunch of kids. We loved it. This was war game heaven. The event was heralded by all the dogs in town. My parents were angry, but what was I supposed to do? Sesame Street hadn't been invented yet, and even if it had been, who had a television set? Who even knew it existed? What did that have to do with us, anyway? We were happy "stealing" a ride.

The best activity of all was swimming in the lake. Well, it could have been the best activity if only I could swim. I couldn't for the life of me figure out how to swim, so instead I learned to fake swimming to gain recognition. Staying in shallow water, I would splash with my hands and one leg on the surface of the water, sliding on the other leg on the bottom of the lake. There I was, splashing like a bird in distress, announcing to all that I was indeed swimming. I fooled no one, of course. One day, however, while sliding on my leg, a piece of glass caused a deep gash about an inch below the kneecap. This wound was sewn up; it healed, leaving an impressive scar that was to prove quite a lifesaver once I got to America.

Life's Rituals
(Age 5 to 11)

In the transitional setting of the DP camp, religion and tradition were larger than life. If we were not cleaning up from one holiday, we were preparing for the next one. Besides the holidays, there were weddings galore. People who had postponed their lives during the war were now anxious to start new ones.

I loved weddings. Imagine being able to eat all you wanted. There was also plenty of soda and wine. The wine was homemade from grapes, raisins, or plums. It was mostly for rituals; not too potent, but enough to make me one jovial kid. Children weren't offered wine, but I could always collect the leftovers from other cups of wine and make one full glass.

On one occasion I concocted a potion from the remains of everyone's drinking glasses and offered it to an aunt of mine. Her child was seriously ill in the hospital. I handed her the glass with the proclamation "To your child's recovery" and told her that she now had to finish the glass for her child to recover. She thanked me for the blessing and asked me where I had gotten the drink. I told her. I remember her look of disgust as she reluctantly drank it all up.

I felt that her anger toward me during the next few weeks was totally unwarranted. The concoction didn't seem that repugnant, and besides, her child did recover. All right, so I tried to see if I could control an adult using superstition. Didn't they do that all the time - that is, control me (and each other) the same way?

Our DP camp had a distinct social order and hierarchy. The people who did not rigorously follow the rituals were criticized by those who were more observant and thus had some power to control. The social pecking order was clearly connected to the degree of Jewish devotion and observance one practiced. We all lived on top of each other, with nowhere to hide. Those who were otherwise more liberal of mind were thus pressured into the appearance of observance.

One time my father took me to the big city of Ulm, Germany. I saw the tall buildings, department stores, toys. I had a wonderful day with my dad. We were about to go home when I spotted a magnificent, mysterious structure. My father told me it was the Munster Kirche, a centuries-old church that spiraled into the sky. I asked if we could enter the church. My father said yes, looked in every direction to make sure we weren't noticed, and quickly ushered me in. We climbed up the carved spiral stairs to the very top. This was a truly awesome structure.

I still remember how when we left, my father reminded me, "You must not utter a word about entering a church to anyone at the DP camp."

As we stepped off the church's street corner, we simultaneously turned back and, in a conditioned reflex, uttered "pooh, pooh, pooh" as we spat three times in quick succession on the pavement. We proceeded forward, neither of us looking back. I didn't have to be taught to spit. I had already learned this Jewish custom at the earliest age, as a way to cleanse an irreligious act, to overcome the devil.

The church was forbidden, yet it was a thing of great beauty and grace. In some sense it foretold a recurring future theme of my life - seeking the forbidden.

I often played at the trolley station. My favorite pastime was to place German pennies on the trolley tracks and, after the trolley had passed over them, retrieve them, flattened. Those machines we see at penny arcades that squeeze a penny, flatten it, and emboss a prayer or some such thing on it, I am sure were invented by one of my playmates at the DP camp.

On weekdays I could play at the trolley station to my heart's content, but on the Sabbath all these Jewish people from camp kept chasing me away. (Religious Jews are not allowed to ride a trolley or any other vehicle on the Sabbath.) "Go back to camp, Srulic, what are you doing here? Don't do that, little boy, it's dangerous. Besides, it's Sabbath, you little goy (Gentile)." I would keep on playing, and a little while later another Jewish man from DP camp would bend over and express his concern or disapproval.

Finally I became suspicious about all their expressed concern. These were the same people who wouldn't save my life when I almost missed the train, how come they're so intent on saving my soul? I wondered. Why did so much of their concern for my safety become evident only on Saturdays? I also wondered why all these people appeared two stations away from camp. I was there so that my parents wouldn't find me engaging in this disapproved-of activity, but why were they there?

One Sabbath when I was urged to go home by a DP camp member, I pretended to do so, but instead remained to observe him. To my surprise, this very same man that had just a moment before scolded me for acting like a little goy now himself boarded the trolley on Sabbath. I remained at my post and noticed that there were others from camp who did the same thing. They walked two stations away from camp and mounted the trolley with less risk of being observed by other Jews. I soon realized that the reason I was a source of annoyance was that with me there, they would have to walk a station or two further from camp so as not to be observed. I also noticed that if two Jews passed each other near the station, each pretended that the other did not exist. People from the DP camp were very easy to identify. On Sabbath they were clean and neat, but nevertheless were definitely not dressed for a Vogue photo session.

Seeing these people pretending to be religious and fooling each other made me skeptical. I saw the hypocrisy and rebelled against religion from my earliest days.

Early Education
(Age 5 to 11)

The older kids had more options. My sister, who was twelve years old when we arrived in Germany, was considered old enough (though barely) to commute to school by train. She left the DP camp each morning and traveled by rail to a fine school in Munich for the seven years we spent in Germany. There she received a well-rounded education and became fluent in German and English.

Some effort was made to offer a little education to the younger children in the camps. At times, the more educated among the adults would volunteer to conduct some makeshift classes. As it was all perceived to be temporary anyway, it was a very feeble, unstructured effort. The classes, when they did exist, were crude, boring and rowdy. This was a totally impossible environment for me. It was formalized chaos and I had had enough chaos. The classes were disorganized. As I hardly understood anything anyway, and it was so easy to escape, I did.

At first I just did not want to go, so I didn't. As time went on however, classes lost their transient nature and began to be viewed by the camp as something permanent. At this time parental pressure increased. I would have to go to school.

As fortune had it, however, I broke my leg in a sledding accident and was confined to my home in a cast for months. Then there was some kind of reshuffling and we changed camps. A new disorder allowed me to elude school again. Then I broke my leg a second time, this time more seriously. Back in a cast in the house again. The doctors said that in view of the amount of time my leg had now been in a cast it would probably not grow as much as the other leg, and that I would most likely walk with a limp forever. When the cast came off, I did limp, but only for a while.

My parents' anxiety grew to desperation. I was getting older and was still completely illiterate, and now I also walked with a limp. As a last chance to give me some education, they enrolled me in the first grade in a German public school. The classes were taught in German. My understanding of spoken Yiddish made it possible to follow along in class.

The school was spotless and highly structured. The children were squeaky clean and nicely clothed. The war was well over, and the Jews and the Germans could now be friends and like each other. But German children weren't yet debriefed, so I had to suffer name-calling and various other abuses on the way home from school.

After the first week in the German school my parents were summoned by the teacher and advised that every few moments I ran up to the blackboard, looked at it and returned to my seat. Perhaps an eye exam was in order.

My parents agreed and made an appointment for me with an ophthalmologist.

I was prepared for the ophthalmologist for weeks before the appointment date. I knew I was going to see a very big doctor in Munich. I knew we'd be going there by train and that he was very important, which of course was why we had to wait that long for an appointment.

What an adventure. This train had cushioned seats and big clean windows, too. Munich was still not rebuilt from the war. There were still many bombed-out buildings, but they seemed so tidy. It was as if the bombs knew they were landing in Germany and expected to cause destruction, but in a tidy manner.

After sitting in the ophthalmologist's waiting room for over an hour, I was directed into the big doctor's office. He seemed bigger than the statues of Stalin that I remembered from Russia. Most startling of all, however, was that he was black. He was completely black - very black. I had never seen a black man before. I didn't know such existed. Initially I was afraid of this man. I don't know what language he spoke, but it didn't matter. It wouldn't be a language I knew. He just motioned at things and made himself understood. He was very gentle and I quickly forgot about my fear. It was very clear to me that this is what a big important ophthalmologist must look like. It was well worth waiting four weeks to see him.

My vision was corrected with spectacles. The world appeared quite different to me with my first pair of glasses. This discovery explained at once my lack of any ability or interest in school. I could not clearly see what was written on the page in front of me without eyeglasses.

As a result of the spectacles, the adults in the DP camp dubbed me "Professor." This was painful to me, since I thought the extent of my illiteracy was quite apparent to all, not just to me. I wasn't so ignorant as not to realize that I was illiterate. When someone called me Professor I took it as a direct attack on my illiteracy. As there was much idleness in camp, everything served as an amusement, and everyone had time to tease me about looking like a little professor. I'll show them, I thought. I will become a professor some day and will show them all. Yes, I'll be in charge of a big class and all these people will sit in my class and I'll make them all wear glasses. I'll have a class full of pupils with glasses and they'll all bump into each other and I'll laugh, and in turn call each of them "Professor."

I remained in that school for two months and learned the German alphabet before we moved again to another camp and schooling got interrupted once more. As it turned out, the two months in the German school was the only education I received until the age of twelve, when I started school again in the U.S.

The bulk of my education had to come from the streets, the camps, the bazaar, the trains, "stealing the border" and the occasional movies that were shown in camp.

The DP camp was supported by various government agencies and augmented by private charitable organizations. From CARE, we received packages that contained life's essentials like Spam, Carnation milk, coffee and hefty amounts of chunky chocolate. The Red Cross, on the other hand, supplied us with toothbrushes and toothpaste, presumably to rid our teeth of the milk-soaked, coffee-stained, chocolate-covered Spam that CARE gave us.

These agencies also dispensed food for our minds. Since most of us were likely to go to America, every now and then some agency would offer a lecture on American culture, or a movie on American life, so that we would know what to expect. Typical of the type of movie seen was Francis the Talking Mule, with Donald O'Connor, filmed at West Point Military Academy (a setting like the Princeton University campus), or movies with starlets riding ponies and driving cars on some lush ranch in Kentucky.

To say I knew no English at all would not be correct. On the other hand, how much English can you learn from a mule? In some of the lectures on American life, we were taught some popular American songs. Among those songs was "My Hat It Has Three Corners." I learned that song well. In case it ever came up in America, I wanted to be well prepared.

Sex
(1950 - age 10)

The first time my leg broke, it was my own fault. Mere sledding down the hill had become boring, so creating a caravan by tying several sleds together seemed the natural thing to do. My sled was the caboose, the rationale being that all the sleds pulling would increase the speed. While going downhill, the sleds began to snake out of control. While I was trying to slow down, my leg somehow got caught under the sled. The other sleds dragged me into the side of a tree, causing the break, and then proceeded to drag me down to the bottom of the hill.

When my leg broke in this sledding accident, my mother looked for reassurance from the doctor that the break would heal strongly. The doctor assured her that it would. In fact, he said, the healing process would cause calcium deposits to be formed, which would make that part of the leg so strong that it would never break again.

A few years after this first break, during an excursion to Munich, my parents were looking in a store window while I played on top of a mound of ice. Suddenly a police car pulled over and the police got out in hot pursuit of someone. A German shepherd leaped out of the police car to join the chase. I was in the path of the dog. The dog charged into me, causing me to fall and break my leg again. This time it wasn't my fault, but it was just as painful nevertheless.

All I could think about on the way to the hospital was the doctor's promise that it wouldn't break again. X-rays proved the doctor technically correct. The doctor was quick to point out that the breaks were in different places. In fact he seemed very proud that the former breaks, the ones he had guaranteed, were not involved at all.

The second break warranted a long stay in a big German city hospital. Since I had no radio or TV and was unable to read or write, the weeks at the hospital dragged on. My parents, aware of my plight, bought me a most elaborate erector set. After building everything imaginable, I still had many hours of boredom left to deal with.

If everything in life has a purpose, then the reason I broke my leg the second time must have been so that I could begin my sex education.

Sharing my hospital room was another little boy and a pretty little blond girl, both German and my age. My Yiddish had to be stretched severely so that I could socialize with these kids in German. (The two languages have similarities.) The effort was well worth it.

During the nights the nurse turned on a nightlight. There was no supervision. Within a few days I learned to communicate sufficiently to lure the little girl into my bed. It was instinctual.

In the DP camp, when animals in heat carried on, older kids as well as some adults hovered around them and goaded them on, giving significance to the event. I suspected that humans engaged in something similar. In any case I had a remarkable attraction to the little blond girl. I was curious and drawn to her for reasons that I couldn't understand.

As I was in a cast from my toes to halfway up my thigh, I could not manage to orchestrate much further experimentation. After a few nights of trying, I gave up.

Still curious about the nature of this whole mystery however, I achieved partial satisfaction by becoming a consultant. I urged the blond girl to go over to the bed of the other little boy. This boy was not as socially gregarious as I was. On the other hand, he was not physically hampered by a cast. I proceeded to direct activities between them. I had no idea what or why, guided only by instinct that told me something was possible here. Move over, Dr. Ruth.

The United States: Atlantic Crossing
(1951 - age 11)

Finally, after seven years of waiting in camps, we got word we were going to America. My grandparents would not be leaving with us. By then, my grandfather had passed away, and my grandmother had emigrated to Israel, to live out the rest of her life in the Holy land.

The last few weeks prior to leaving Germany were busy ones. In anticipation of our migration, much had to be done. Everyone had some idea as to which commodities were in desperate short supply in America and thus stocked up on what they hoped would be good investments. What little money people had was put into buying watches, silverware, cameras and table top clocks with rotating weights or pendulums enclosed in a glass dome.

On the morning of our departure, there was last-minute packing to do, final documents to be stamped, and yes, perhaps we hadn't bought enough watches.

Few people had any wealth, but everyone had possessions. Certainly we'll need those pillows, and bedding, and cooking utensils in the U.S. Everyone had crates full of stuff.

On our last day in Germany my father decided to take me out for the day. Just the two of us. After all, I was practically a teenager, give or take a year. We went to a beer garden and each had a stein of beer. My father and I, two men about town.

Afterward, we strolled along and Father bought me a pair of plastic binoculars with a magnification power of at least 2. These binoculars, we both agreed, would be very useful in sighting America and examining the fine details of the land prior to disembarking from the ship.

It was a small ship, the S.S. General Stuart, a military personnel transport. The dormitory had bunks that were stacked four high, held by two hinges on one side and a chain on the other. We would sleep exactly like soldiers, as we were in their dormitories. To us, it was the Waldorf Astoria. It was taking us to America!

It was only the second day of the three-week journey, and it seemed that every adult on the ship was seasick. The ship was small, and it bobbed up and down in the turbulent Atlantic. The perimeter of the ship was lined with adults who stood there day and night heaving overboard.

This was my first clue that things might not be exactly as I had seen in the camp movies. One of the movies shown in the DP camp depicted the Queen Mary, its passengers dressed in beautiful outfits, playing shuffleboard, swimming in the deck pools, and eating gracious meals at the captain's table. I searched for those amenities on our ship, but only for the briefest time. I began to suspect that perhaps America wasn't all milk and honey with gold in the streets after all.

During our journey we encountered a severe storm. I don't know if it was a result of some damage, or a safety measure, but the ship began to list severely. Ropes were tied all along the outside for people to hold onto as they negotiated their way from the dorm to the mess hall, or to the bathrooms.

The ship's dizzying motion seemed to have little if any effect on the children or the military personnel, who, I suspect, were conditioned to it.

Limping from level to level, I played or spent hours next to the Coca-Cola dispensing machine. Soldiers would walk up, insert a nickel, and a cup would drop as Coca-Cola poured into it. Sometimes a cup failed to drop properly, and the Coca-Cola would spill out. I was amazed, stunned, by this piece of machinery. If a soldier passed within eyeshot of my station alongside the Coke machine, I would volunteer to insert his nickel for him and return with his Coke. The Queen Mary might have had Xavier Cugat's whole band, but watching the miracle of this Coca-Cola dispensing machine was sufficient entertainment for me.

When the ship began to lean, nature acted as a great equalizer. Everybody limped, in a manner of speaking, not just me. Now I was the same as everyone else. In fact, I thought that if I walked in a certain direction, the tilt offset my condition and perhaps I walked even better than the others. I dedicated myself to walking up and down the ship deck and kept checking to see if my walk had improved. I don't really know where it happened but by the time I put my feet on U.S. soil, my limp, which was already on its way to recovery, had disappeared completely.

The ship kept tilting, the storm kept storming, the adults kept throwing up. The situation didn't appear promising. I didn't know if the ship would make it, and I had great doubts about my parents surviving the trip. They looked awful as they leaned against the rail throwing up for the third straight week in a row.

I asked my parents to write down the address of my aunt in America, as I was certain by now that I would be orphaned. I memorized this address and learned from the soldiers how to ask for directions in "good" English.

Hardly anyone could sleep on the night preceding the morning of our arrival. We knew that sometime during the dawn we would enter the port of New York. I was at the rail fiercely focusing my power 2 binoculars all night, waiting to catch my first glance of America.

It must have been five in the morning with a hint of day entering the sky when I spotted something. A faint light. The light grew in intensity as we approached New York harbor. I could fully see the majesty of the Statue of Liberty lighting the way to land.

I had heard of the Statue of Liberty, in America, but when I saw her, it looked as if she had stepped into the sea to greet me, instead of standing on land. It was as if she was as anxious to see me as I was to see her. She exuded a feminine peacefulness, yet there was a masculine strength about her. She also appeared so rested, as if she had gotten there way before we had and had already recuperated from the trip.

I was glad to see her. She was the only one around me not throwing up. For that alone she could be held in high esteem. With everyone around me looking as if they weren't going to survive the last few miles of the trip, I found solace in her reassuring face. She was a definite survivor. She looked so calm, she must have known that it was safe here.

I don't think that a person born in America could ever see her the way she looked to me that morning as she grew out of the sea. Nor, for that matter, the way she still looks to me to this day.

The romantic approach past the Statue of Liberty belied the experience that awaited us immediately on the west side of New York. Disembarking took hours. I stood in the front of the ship with a view of the West Side shipping terminal and the adjacent streets. I couldn't understand it. Was there a war in the U.S., too? If there wasn't a war here, how could it look more chaotic and disheveled than bombed-out Munich? I was certain that there was some explanation, but the adults couldn't be disturbed, as they were too busy finding their relatives, registering with the proper assistance agencies, arranging where to sleep that night, etc.

Our first night in the U.S. was to be spent at my aunt's house in Brooklyn. This was the same aunt that breast fed me in Russia. Her immigration to the U.S. preceded ours by a year or so. By the time we arrived, she was practically an American. She guided our first footsteps on this soil directly to the subway station.

Who are all these people in the subway station speaking so loudly, laughing uncontrollably? In the crowd I hear strange sounds, and a recurring expression: "Hey, mother—er, hey, mother—er". And a Chinese family, speaking in sounds that were even more strange than English. And look over there, could it be? Does this land have that many ophthalmologists?

The subway screeched frighteningly. As we moved along, it got more and more crowded. An elderly lady entered the subway. I, being the youngest, knew it was my duty to vacate my seat for her. I proceeded to rise. Whether it was her disbelief that I was getting up, or her fear that I would have a change of heart, she made a mad dash for my seat, knocking me down in the process. This country is different, I thought to myself. I couldn't understand it. I had been told that the Germans were barbaric. Yet outwardly the Germans appeared more civilized than these first Americans I encountered.

Our screechy subway ride ended in the East New York section of Brooklyn. The area was more appealing than the shipping terminal, but it was a far cry from the land depicted in Francis The Talking Mule, nor did it even faintly resemble anything like a lush Kentucky farm. The America that had been represented to us by well-meaning American social workers in Germany and the America that I was to experience for the next fifteen years were not the same. It was puzzling. I wondered for some time whether my parents had been offered a checklist of places in America to arrive at. Did this checklist accidentally leave out places like Scarsdale? As I got to know America, I concluded that the West Side harbor was definitely not the place to admit first-time arrivals if America wanted to make the best impression.

Once we entered my aunt's apartment, we were impressed. She had a living room, two bedrooms, an eat-in kitchen that she didn't have to share with anyone, and a bathroom inside the apartment. She even had a refrigerator and a television.

We all marveled at the apartment while exchanging family stories. Most of all, we received important tips that helped to acclimate us to American ways, including which words we must avoid. Immigrants typically learned English piecemeal. They learned the English for certain nouns, but for the longest time they merged these with Yiddish or Polish verbs. For instance, the Yiddish word for shake or pour is "shit." An immigrant who wanted some salt on his plate could produce the expression, "Please shit on me a little."

The other thing that my aunt cautioned us about was the nature of salutations in this country. In particular, she told us that if an American asked us how we were, we were to just say okay. She said not to tell them anything specific, because they don't really want to know. She warned us that an American asks you how you are and keeps on walking. In fact, she said, they often answer the question themselves, saying, "How are you? Fine!" This was a novel concept to us, for, in our heritage, if someone asked you how you were, he meant it, and you actually told him everything: The children are well, the kidney is acting up, etc.

The evening was highly instructional. We kept learning such interesting details. My startled parents would take turns protesting disbelief.

"You don't say, you don't say," they kept repeating.

But my sister, who was now almost eighteen years old and the family authority on the English language was quick to reassure my parents that my aunt was correct.

This brief education, however, still did not protect me from formulating such fine English expressions in the street as "How much is the clock?" which is a literal translation of the Yiddish for "What time is it?"

It took some years of playing in the street, going to school and watching TV before I developed any English skills. I imitated a great deal from TV. It could be Shakespearean, or Western - it was all

English to me. Many of my finest expressions were lifted right from the mouth of Wild Bill Hickock or Hopalong Cassidy. It all sounded like perfectly good English to me. Yup, Wild Bill and I, why we sounded just like pardners for a short spell there, except that every now and then a Shakespearean word could creep into the same sentence. How was I to know the difference?

Dwelling for the first few weeks was provided to us by HIAS (Hebrew Immigrant Aid Society). The housing was in a sleazy S.R.O. type hotel on Broadway.

My education started in the streets of lower Broadway. I was small for my age and wore big spectacles and strange-looking hand-me-downs. I picked up enough English words to survive. "Throw ball," "look big tits," etc. Kids traded baseball cards, and insisted on knowing if I was a Dodger or Yankee fan. I had no idea what a Dodger fan was, or why I had to be one.

It was all so alien, but I was getting the grasp of it. There were new observations every day. On one occasion, I shared my newfound knowledge with my sister. "America isn't that complicated," I told her. "If you want money, you say trick or treat. If you

want someone to leave you alone, you say f—k you."
Some country!

None of my old names seemed to work for me. The kids couldn't pronounce most of them. I was envious. American kids had such nice names, like Tom, Butch, Lou, Mike. I needed a new name befitting my new country. Outside my window I had a view of Joe's Bar and Grill. Joe, I thought, like Joe DiMaggio (whoever he was). That's a good name for me. This way, no one will suspect I am foreign. While we were registering for green cards (preceding citizenship) and the official asked me my name, I responded loud and clear, "Joe Rais." My parents just looked at each other and shrugged. As I got older, I regretted this choice and thought that the only name that could have been less fitting for me than the name I had picked was "Grill."

Possessions
(1952 - age 12)

By our second month in this country, both my parents found factory jobs. My father's skill at running the small utility company in Poland qualified him for a minimum-wage job sewing brassieres. My mother found similar work. With both working, it became possible for us to move into our own apartment near my aunt.

It was a small dilapidated apartment on the first floor of a four-story walk up. We painted, cleaned and scrubbed. My mother hung curtains and it was home. For the first time in my life, I lived in an apartment that was not shared by aunts, uncles and cousins. We now had two bedrooms of our own. My parents had one bedroom, my sister had the other, and I got to sleep on a small couch in the living room. I got the best room, for it soon held our first American possession: the television.

The neighborhood was poor, but everyone, it seemed, had possessions. Every American home had a television, many kids had a 45 rpm record player, and a few kids even had portable radios. All these new things to be had - oh yes, some country!

The things we brought from Europe, all those watches, cameras and silver we bought and brought with us, the things that we packed and unpacked and repacked and guarded and sometimes smuggled through borders, those possessions that weighed us down, those things that we possessed and that ultimately possessed us - the pawn stores were full of them. If there ever was a shortage of those items it was surely remedied by the influx of the few hundred thousand immigrants that had arrived here before us. It didn't seem that anyone was in the market for watches with the brand name Doxa. We all had possessions, but they were the wrong kind.

For the adults, their European possessions became the relics of their disillusionment. The relics of the American dream, of the gold in the streets. The dream that America would open its arms to us. The dream that America was waiting for us did not materialize for many. America was not waiting for us or our possessions. It had enough immigrants in the streets and enough Doxa watches in the pawn shops.

I wanted possessions too. I didn't even consider asking for them. My parents used to talk about how in three more weeks they could afford to buy me some warmer pants for the winter. Dare I ask for a record player?

I was already twelve years old, and had long since learned to be self-reliant. We lived one block from a neighborhood market. There were outdoor fruit carts, clothing stores, pawn shops, used electric appliance stores and junk stores of all kinds. Even the trash that one could find in the street was very rich. Imagine, Americans threw out broken television sets, old phonographs, malfunctioning typewriters. Didn't they realize that an old television set contained speakers that could be reused, or at least taken apart to retrieve magnets? Look at all these tubes. I could clean all these tubes out, test them, and put them in my inventory. I bet the local TV repairman can use this 12AU7 tube. For me the streets did seem paved with gold.

Here as in Azerbaijan I gravitated to the street market, and here too the vendors in the street knew me very well. They knew when I was looking for a part of some kind and likewise, I knew if they needed anything. I was willing to build or repair anything. One store needed some light fixture to be replaced, another store needed some additional shelving to be built, or perhaps some new display in the window. It wasn't long before I had my own phonograph. It was homebuilt, of course, from remnant parts, didn't look elegant, played only 78 rpm records, but it worked just the same. I learned to build almost anything I needed, and if I couldn't build it, I could barter for it.

I wanted roller skates so bad, but couldn't find anyone willing to part with theirs. I located a kid with only one skate, who was willing to trade it for some magnets that I had recovered from discarded speakers. One skate was only half a conquest, but would suffice for the time being. I trained my right foot to skate quite well, and then my left foot. It was years before I had the opportunity to skate with both feet at the same time.

The market was a familiar place. It felt like Azerbaijan. I still had vivid memories of the merchants trading yard goods. The Azerbaijanis would measure yardage as the distance between their hand and their nose. I used to wonder if profitable partnerships were ever formed between two men, one with short arms to do the selling and another with long arms to do the purchasing.

The biggest difference between the market in Azerbaijan and the market on Blake Avenue in the East New York section of Brooklyn was that in this marketplace almost everyone spoke Yiddish.

At the market, in the streets, at home, or anywhere else we socialized, we spoke only Yiddish, so progress in learning English was slow. This stalled my education.

The Return to Formal Education
(1952 - age 12)

The biggest problem was my education, or rather the lack of it. I was already twelve years old, and all in all I had only had a few months of schooling in my whole life. I couldn't read or write in any language. I knew how to speak Yiddish, write the German alphabet, sing a few songs that nobody ever sang, and mouth a few words that I learned from a talking mule.

The school officials decided that it would be better to place me with kids close to my own age, rather than to place me in the first grade, which is where I belonged. I consequently found myself in the sixth grade for the remaining few months of the semester.

Usually I just sat at my desk and listened. I would understand a word here and there. Sometimes the teacher placed me in the back with Helena, the star pupil. There Helena would teach me the alphabet. Helena was so smart and beautiful, and I had such a crush on her. I couldn't wait for the days that I got to sit next to Helena at that small student desk, with our bodies touching. How can I get her to like me, when I can hardly speak to her?

One day as she was going through a grader with me, she pointed to a picture of a piano and told me she had a piano. I pointed out that I was familiar with that word and that I could play the piano. This was not true, of course. I liked her and was fishing for an invitation to her house. She invited me to come over some day the following week. Meanwhile, I prepared to impress her and with the help of a distant American cousin who owned a piano, I learned to play "Three Blind Mice."

I visited her house and skillfully gave my performance. She reciprocated and played "Fur Elise" in return. I sat adoringly next to her. Wishing to compliment her, I said, "You smell." Of course, this was not exactly what I meant. In Yiddish the expression meant that she smelled very nice. She didn't express much interest in me after that, and I was never sure if it was my craft at the keyboard or my gift for gab.

On one occasion while visiting the bathroom at school I was confronted by two kids.

"Hey, what's that you got, man?" He was referring to my watch.

"This is my clock," I answered proudly while pointing to my watch.

"Yeah, what kind is it? Show it to us." I took it off and showed it to them. They examined it, thanked me, and started to leave. As I protested, they asked me what I was going to do about it. I attacked fiercely, knocked down the boy wearing my watch, and recovered it. The other boy, apparently startled by my retaliation, stood there paralyzed for a second. Then they both ran off, muttering.

When school let out these kids appeared again. This time they were backed up by a whole gang. They kept provoking me and pushing one another into me and repeatedly asking me, "What kind of mother—er are you, man?" Since I didn't know the correct answer, they kept on pushing me and I kept inching my way toward home. One kid kept placing something on his shoulder and daring me to knock the chip off his shoulder. The other kids pushed me into him, to help things along. I didn't know about the chip-off-the-shoulder business, but surmised that this was some American ritual that would give him license to beat me up.

I was trapped. It was clear they were going to beat me up. I didn't think it was possible to escape them; then I remembered that I had some swords that I had previously traded for. I yelled out, "Enough, we settle this like in my country!"

"What?" they exclaimed. "What are you talking about?"

"Okay," I said. "Duel to death."

"What?"

"To death! I bring swords!" They all followed me to my house. I went in knowing I had to go out again or face the same situation the following day. I came out with two swords, confronted the biggest bully, and said, now with a heavier German accent,

"Duel to death!"

"Did you ever duel before?" the bully asked me.

"Yes, many time. Look!" I said as I uncovered the scar I still had on my leg from the swimming accident. "See! He cut me! I killed him!"

The kids did not know what to make of this. I must have appeared quite peculiar to them... a foreigner, clothed strangely, crazy enough to hit a gang member. They decided I was too unpredictable and did not stay around to see if I was bluffing.

They never bothered me again. A few more months passed and I moved on from grade school. The requirements for moving on to junior high school? Well, I'm not sure there were any requirements. Everyone moved ahead. However, once in junior high school, the students were tracked according to accomplishment, or capability. In my achievement tests as well as my IQ test (administered in English), I ranked someplace below where the graph began. There was no argument that I belonged in the slowest classes. These classes were also home to the school's trouble makers.

Hoods

(1952 - age 12)

Some of the kids were gang members, others retained their independence. They were all problem kids of some kind, with no shred of interest in schooling. They were just putting in time, and would do anything for amusement. They heckled the teacher, stuck safety pins into each other, and me, for comic relief. They were all bigger than I was. My lack of English comprehension made me a favorite target.

The only saving grace was that I was so small, I wasn't perceived as much of a prize. Unless it was raining heavily there would almost always be a fight after school let out. I learned to meander carefully between the bullies and the gangs. Somehow I must have amused the most vicious bullies to the extent that they allowed me to live for my entertainment value. Every so often I would be challenged by some other lowly kid who needed a dog to kick. With those, I held my own.

The classroom was a battlefield. The teacher was readily identifiable as the least commanding individual in the classroom. If this wasn't the result of being petrified by the armed and dangerous students, then he was lethargic because of the general hopelessness of the educational system and my class in particular.

The students knew that whether they put in work or not, they would be promoted to the next grade with the obligatory 65% mark, so no one bothered to do any work. The teacher, however, still tried to follow his curriculum. As best as I can recall, the requirements were as follows:

In English you had to know the difference between "to," "too," and "two," also between "weather" and "whether." In math you had to figure out how much to pay for an article if it was discounted 15%.

A passing grade in history required that you know that there were two Senators for each state, but that in the House of Representatives, representation was in proportion to the state's population.

I learned all of this in the seventh grade, then again in the eighth grade, and once more in the ninth grade. I never misuse "to," "too," "two," "whether" or "weather." If I ever do, it's not me, it's my word processor. (Honest.)

Unfortunately, it was presumed by the school system that the students in our classes had neither the ability to learn nor to retain any knowledge, and the students obliged, making it a self-fulfilling prophecy.

Our rigorous academic training was supplemented by a wide variety of offerings in shop class. We had wood working, metal working, cooking, etc. My first experience was in cooking. On the first day of class the students were asked to stand against the rear wall, as the instructor began her introduction.

The teacher pointed at me and said, "You, you over there. Come here and bring your pots." I stood frozen.

"You," she repeated. "Come over here with your pots." I didn't move. "Come on, let's see your pots."

The word pots in Yiddish means "dick." I was recalling the last time I showed it to someone - they snipped off a piece. Besides, the days of my showing it on command had long passed. Is this woman crazy?

I just stood there looking bewildered for a while until she gave up on me and directed herself to another student. Such was my life in junior high school.

School Gym
(1952 - age 12)

This was where the fantastic locker room stories were spun. I listened with great interest as the boys boasted of their conquests. I didn't know whether to believe them. I knew Jewish boys didn't do that, but these boys weren't Jewish. They probably did anything they wanted. I couldn't imagine their mothers yelling at them. Their mothers were probably afraid to yell at them. I saw them as killers.

Even though they were my age, they were so much bigger. They were bigger than my father. These American kids grew big. The kids in my classes were tough and mean creeps. But their stories were exciting.

Nick boasted how Angela did it with him. He described everything with the greatest detail. I listened very intently. Nick was the strongest and also the most despicable kid in my class. He was the head bully of my class and had some stature with the neighborhood street gangs as well. You didn't expect much wisdom to stream out of Nick's mouth. However, when it came to sex or violence, Nick was an undisputed authority. Violence didn't interest me, but when Nick spoke about sex, I listened. Ordinarily I wouldn't believe anything he said, but these things rang true. He confirmed my suspicion that people did do it. Not only dogs, but people did it too. "F" wasn't just a curse word. And people didn't do just that either. There was this oral business. It's hard to believe... and... and... and the guys "come," and girls also can "come," and girls can get real hot, and they want it, and sometimes they won't let go? It all sounded semi-disgusting at first.

But then I too began visualizing doing these things with Angela. It must be normal. Every kid knew about it. These kids used to play pranks on me and fool me. But this must be true - they couldn't all be conspiring to lie to me. Kids outside of my classes spoke about it too. Their stories were consistent.

Get a load of this, the most important information of all, and I learn it from stupid Nick. My father was right when he told me you can learn something from everybody. My father always lectured me to be attentive to everybody. If I was restless when someone spoke, he would tell me to listen and pay attention, that I would learn something.

Once when I was younger I protested. We were in the street, and some neighbor engaged my father in a conversation. It was boring, and I wanted to continue walking wherever it was we were going. I nagged my father and annoyed him. When the neighbor finally went away my father yelled at me, "Why can't you stand still and listen?"

"Dad," I insisted, "the man is stupid. Why should I have to listen to him?"

"Because you'll learn something."

"What can I learn from a stupid man?" I asked.

"You can learn something from everybody."

"Even from a stupid man?"

"Yes, son, from anybody. Son," he said, "even a broken watch is correct twice a day."

This made quite an impression on me. I could visualize this broken watch lying in the street, crushed, with its arms set at two o'clock. And sure enough, it did tell the right time at two in the morning and at two at night. I couldn't argue with that logic. Even a broken watch is correct twice a day, so I suppose even a total fool could say something right, or meaningful.

I daydreamed about what I would give in this world to touch Angela's breast. Whenever I saw Angela, she looked so sexy with the bra outline showing under her sweater. I watched her moving her lips and cracking gum. I couldn't stop thinking of her. Nick, that scar-faced gangster, if he knew what I was thinking, he'd kill me for sure.

On certain days we had dancing classes in gym. We lined up single file - boys on one side, girls on the other. Accordingly, we would wind up with a partner for dancing. One time I wound up with Angela. Angela embraced me and wore me like a coat for the entire dance. I was age twelve. My erection was rubbing into her. Yet I was embarrassed, and somewhat fearful. Will Nick know? Will she tell him? Will he kill me? Angela didn't seem to mind it, though. She wrapped herself firmly around me and kept grinding to the song "Earth Angel." It didn't happen then, but she led me to it. I understood. That night I rubbed myself and discovered what can happen. I couldn't wait for the next time we had dancing in gym.

Every time we had gym I calculated how to enter the line so that I would wind up with Angela. When Angela danced with me it was almost like a tease, as if she were saying, "Don't you wish you Jewish boys were allowed to do that too?" Oh yes, yes, I wish, I wish. She never said a word after the dance. She just thanked me politely.

Earth Angel, Earth Angel. Oh how I wished I had a 45 rpm phonograph and that record. I would have played it all night long and masturbated and thought of Angela, or the little girl in the German hospital. If she were only here now, I thought. Imagine, I had her in my hands, that smooth body and long blond hair, and she did anything I asked of her. That was such a close one. Our parts were actually touching! I wondered if I would ever be so lucky again. Damn that broken leg!

Friend Alvin
(1952 - age 12)

I couldn't form a friendship with any of the hoods from my classes. I just coped with them. I made other friends in the street. Alvin was one of the first kids I met in this country. I don't quite remember how we met, but we became friends. Alvin was a diligent, energetic, if somewhat hyperactive kid. He had many interests and hobbies. He didn't seem to mind telling me about all of them, even though I didn't understand a word. Alvin also formed a club, of which I was a member. I have no recollection if the club had any purpose other than to play, but I recall that Alvin dominated it, and that he was careful to follow and quote Robert's Rules of Order frequently. I had no idea what Robert's Rules of Order were, and neither did the other kids, I'm sure. But Alvin knew.

Alvin needed to lead, and at the time, I was the ideal follower. I had just arrived off the boat and knew nothing, so I was willing to follow anyone. Well, Alvin knew many things. He knew all the television and radio shows. He knew how to get to the broadcast studios. He knew where and when to stand on line to get the tickets. Alvin also knew who the advertisers of the various shows were, and whether they gave out product samples to the audiences.

On weekends Alvin and I would get up very early in the morning and set off to get those tickets. "No, not there - here. Let's go to this show. Their sponsor is a tuna fish company and they will probably give samples of tuna fish." Alvin was right. We would come home with cans of tuna, bars of soap, toothpaste, and such. When I got home, my booty created some excitement. It was like opening a CARE package at the DP camp all over again.

One day we were in the audience of a live TV show. This particular TV show was a debate show. The guests were discussing some important world event. I had no idea what they were talking about. In the second part of the show the cameras turned to the audience for questions. Alvin had a question and one of the panel members responded to it. I was jealous and wanted to do the same. The problem was that I didn't know what they were talking about!

"Alvin," I whispered, "Make a question for me too." Alvin obliged. He told me what to ask them. I repeated it to him to make sure I had the words right, and raised my hand.

"Yes, you," the show host said, "what is your question?"

I repeated the question very precisely. The show host fielded the question to one of the guests, who discussed it at length, then asked me something in return.

"Alvin, you didn't tell me they do that!" I whispered.

"Yes, and what would you say to that?" the host asked, with the camera zooming in on me.

I saw myself filling up the whole monitor. I had no idea what my original question meant, much less what they were talking about. My foot stepped on Alvin's for assistance, but there was no possibility of escape. The camera was much too close. "Well, what do you think?" he repeated. I smiled feebly into the camera and maintained a frozen posture. Like a squeeze box fully contracted, I could make no sound. The commentator finally decided to move on and the camera moved away from me.

What was to have been the thrill of appearing on TV turned into an embarrassment. My momentary anger with Alvin shortly turned into inward anger at myself. The incident reinforced within me that lying and deception backfire mercilessly. It reminded me that I should not and could not ever depend on someone else to save me. I had to become completely self-reliant. I had to build myself, so that I would not have to depend on some Alvin to save me.

Mortality
(1952 - age 12)

Summer. No school, no percentage calculations to deal with, no cooking classes. My friends and I hitchhiked to the beach every hot day, and every not-so-hot day. It didn't matter. It was the thrill of escaping to a place whose pristine state wasn't as yet destroyed. A piece of land that didn't have buildings from one street corner to the next. Once there, we would swim, play, and search for bottles to return for the deposit money. Finding a few bottles meant being able to take the return trip by subway. Otherwise, we would hitchhike back home as well.

I had learned to swim quite well by then. I also had the mindset of an indestructible teenager. On one clear weekend morning my parents and I were at Brighton Beach. Rockaway Beach seemed only a stone's throw away across the bay. "Why not swim there?" I asked my friend, who was also a good swimmer.

"Great idea!" responded the other indestructible teenager. In we went.

The longer we swam, the larger seemed the separation between Rockaway and Brighton Beach. We stroked relentlessly until we were far enough out that a good-sized fishing vessel passed by. The crew of the boat seemed frantic in their screams. Neither my foreign friend nor I understood what these men were screaming about. The men aboard the vessel surmised that we could not understand English very well and began to make frantic hand signals and screaming, "Sharks." My friend and I soon understood that the boat had grapples behind it, and furthermore, that we were too far out and that there could be sharks in those waters. We knew the word shark, and made a very hasty retreat.

When we got back to the Brighton Beach shoreline we thought that some great disaster had occurred, for the whole beach had converged at the waterline, screaming. As we came in, we realized that we were the cause of the hysteria. When my mother realized we had disappeared into the ocean, she started screaming frantically and summoned all, including the police. My mother was fit to be tied.

She was screaming at me in Yiddish, Polish, Russian, German, English and some words in languages that I didn't understand. Perhaps some Spanish words that she picked up from the Puerto Ricans in the factory where she worked, or even some words in a language that didn't exist. My mother protested in many languages. Often her protest was that the difficulties of living through the Second World War paled in comparison to the difficulties of raising me.

As to making up words that didn't exist, I must confess it was mostly my father who did that. He would say a sentence that otherwise made sense, except for one word. He would often get away with it, because the context would give the meaning of the word. As I got older I confronted him.

"Dad, I know what you mean, but what word is that? Is that a Yiddish word?"

"No!" he would respond.

"Well, then, is it Polish? Is it English?" I would ask.

"No! It's an international word!"

"Dad, there is no such thing!" I proclaimed.

"Sure there is! This word is good in every language, so it's an international word!" he would insist.

I was dumbfounded then, but less so now, for the bottom line was that he did make himself quite well understood by all. Who am I to say there are no international words?

Sometimes it seemed like my mother's sole occupation in life was to make sure I survived into adulthood. As she had saved me in Russia and in Germany, she had to keep on saving me forever. That was her job. She was furious because she had almost failed. It was her job to save me from sharks, from drowning. I made her job so difficult, she was furious at me. My friend and I stood there, out of the water, wet, cold and scared. As it was, we had just been brought down considerably from our pedestal of indestructibility. Yet we had to deal with my mother standing there screaming frantically in "International." We were hoping for a heroes' reception and instead were treated like criminals.

This little round woman with golden teeth was shaking her hand at me. The hand with the simple European wedding band that would never come off, because her fingers were a little too plump and you could see the skin rolling up on each side of the ring. The ring that made her my mother. My protector for life.

Knishes
(1952 - age 12)

The beach was my only escape from the hot humid walk up apartment we lived in. It was freedom. Getting car fare wasn't that difficult, but I also needed other things like soda, ice cream and knishes.

There was a very special place on the boardwalk that made and sold knishes on the premises. The owner made tasty potato, cherry, cheese and other flavor knishes. I saw people trekking up from the beach to buy these knishes, and surmised that I could do business bringing knishes down to them. The owner of the store sold the knishes for twenty cents each. I felt that people would be happy to pay a little more if I brought them right down to their blankets.

I approached the owner and offered to buy knishes from him at a reduced price. "No," he responded, explaining that any sale I made would just cost him a lost sale, so he would in effect be competing against himself. My counter proposal was to sell his knishes at a distance no closer than two beaches from the store. I pointed out that people that far away would not be likely to walk to him anyway, so this would in fact increase his business. He agreed with this logic and we entered a deal where he sold me knishes wholesale at five cents apiece, on condition that I not tell anyone where I got the knishes.

Armed with an initial order of four knishes in a cardboard box, I quickly ran to the agreed-upon territory, yelled out, "Delicious Knishes - 25 cents!" and sold out immediately. I ran back for a dozen more and did the same, ran back for as many as I could carry and did the same. The sun was hot and it was very difficult to walk with shoes on in the sand. Some coins dropped and got lost in the sand, but who cared? It was the end of the day and I had made a lot of money. I was rich, rich, rich!

When I arrived home I summoned a half dozen kids and offered them jobs. I also purchased aprons with coin compartments and painted the words "Hot Knishes" on each. The next day we all went to the beach by subway. I allocated territories to each and arranged meeting places where I would resupply them with knishes. The deal was that I paid them five cents on every knish they sold. Business couldn't have been better. Until...

"Hey you," a voice called. It was a policeman. "Hey, what are you doing?"

"I sell knishes."

"Where did you get them?"

"Grandmother."

"Yeah, your grandmother made them. Where is your grandmother?"

"East New York."

"Still hot," he said as he touched the knishes. "How did you get here so fast?"

"Hitchhike."

"Listen, kid, get off the beach, you can't sell knishes here."

"Okay", I said, then waited until he disappeared and proceeded once more. A half hour later he apprehended me again and yelled, "Hey kid, what's the matter with you? Do I have to arrest you? Hey, do you want to go to jail?"

Suddenly I saw him in a completely different light, standing there so ominous, so tall, with an official uniform and a gun on his hip. Fear overtook me. What am I doing? Am I crazy? I'll be arrested, and maybe sent back to Germany!

"Please, I swear, I no more sell knishes!" I rounded up my staff and returned home. I'm not going back to Germany, uh, uh, not me.

Party Crasher
(1953 - age 13)

My bar mitzvah led to a social awakening. As poor as we were, my parents insisted on a bar mitzvah affair for me. In contrast to our life style, the affair was lavish. The food was plentiful and appetizing. It was also a lot of fun, with music, singing, dancing.

Not only did I get a big party in a hall, with delicious food and presents, but I also discovered some important things.

My affair was held at a catering hall a few blocks from our house. I observed that adults were assigned seats in some planned fashion, but kids were bunched up at an odd table or two. Even though this was a party for me, it seemed that the younger guests were just shoved off to the side. Moreover, I didn't know who some of the guests were, and it occurred to me that not all of them knew me either. This observation proved to be quite useful.

I noticed that the catering hall had functions going on all the time, and I wanted to be part of the parties. A few weeks after my own bar mitzvah party I put on my bar mitzvah suit again and showed up uninvited at someone else's party. When I saw a large enough group enter, I went in with them. An adult directed me to the kiddies' and miscellaneous table. I had no trouble fitting in. I looked like them, dressed like them and spoke like them, so there was no doubt that I belonged there. If the hosts had any doubt, it might have been as to who I belonged to, but they were either too busy, didn't care, or too embarrassed to admit they didn't recognize me.

I would sit at the table, engage in conversation with the other kids, eat the food, dance and have a good time. This became a nice social activity for me, which I repeated occasionally over the next couple of years. I also crashed weddings, and did so with even greater impunity, because at weddings, each side of the family would assume that I belonged to the other side of the family and certainly wouldn't bother me.

As time went on, the novelty of the food wore off, but dancing with the girls became increasingly interesting. I also became quite preoccupied with kissing the bride. Sometimes I managed to kiss the same bride two or three times.

The other thing that became interesting was drinking the wine. For some reason that I don't understand there would be wine at the children's table. They didn't refill those glasses, but they nevertheless were there from the outset of the affair. As I became older, I enjoyed drinking some of that wine. To support that interest, I developed a game. I don't recall the details, but at some point everyone had to pass his wine glass clockwise to the next kid at the table. In this way, I managed to get refills. It's amazing that I did not become an alcoholic!

These parties made me feel good. The environment inside the catering hall shielded me, if only temporarily, from the slums immediately outside. The only problem was, I didn't really belong. I danced with the girls, but couldn't converse freely. I couldn't let them discover that I was a party crasher. As I became more skillful at crashing these parties, I lost my fear and some of the excitement as well. Though I was never caught, I did begin to feel like a fraud, and eventually I stopped doing it. I suppose the management must have caught on to my party crashing but they didn't care. They were probably paid by the head.

Big Revenge
(1955 - age 15)

My sense of self was at best muddled. On the one hand I was resourceful and capable. On the other hand I felt like a total loser. I knew so little. I was in slow classes, surrounded by kids who weren't going anywhere. But I didn't fit in with the nicer kids either, except at dances. With improved nourishment my body had caught up to my age, but I must be so stupid, I thought. And I'm certainly going nowhere.

Even my classmates were going somewhere. One boasted he would become a butcher. Another was going to join his father's business: changing the 45 rpm records in jukeboxes. True, most of them were becoming gangsters, going to reform school, or going to jail. Yet they knew where they were going. I couldn't become a gangster. It wasn't in me. So I was truly going to be a nothing.

My sister, who had been my constant rival from the days in Russia when we both grabbed for the same piece of black bread and sour cream, had always called me an idiot. At the slightest provocation she'd yell, "Mom, keep him away from me! Can't you see he's an idiot?"

Of course she called me an idiot with great authority. After all, she was six years older than I, bright, highly educated, and able to read and write in six languages. By contrast I hadn't yet managed to read or write in a single language with any proficiency.

We may have been raised in the same countries at the same time, but circumstances had dealt each of us a completely different hand. By the time my family left Poland, my sister was six years old and could already read and write Polish and Yiddish. In Russia, she attended school for five years and learned Russian. In Germany she studied in a fine school and learned German and English. She also learned Hebrew after school. This is not to mention the broad education she had in each of these countries.

She knew everything, while I was in slow classes and still could not, indeed had not yet read a single book in any language. If that wasn't enough, she was also considered to be attractive, poised and charming. Who needs a sister like that?

The contrast angered me, and I always found a way to retaliate against her, even though deep down inside I knew that I really was a moron. I often wondered how I wound up in the same family with all these smart people. Was there a mix-up at infancy? After all, it was dark in the forest. Were there other births at the same time? Could they have picked up the wrong infant?

My sister was six years older, and I believed much smarter than I, but I was way more adept technically. We had one television set in the family and had to share it. My parents hardly ever watched it, so it remained for my sister and me to ration it between us. My preference was for shows like "The Cisco Kid," "Hopalong Cassidy," "Gene Autrey," or "The Lone Ranger." My sister's choices were drama, opera, ballets, and talk shows. Conflicts would arise. Her choices often prevailed, as she was able to point out to the judge (my mother) that her choices were by far more worthwhile, compared to what the "idiot" wanted to watch again.

I retaliated by secretly rewiring our television set in such a way that by shifting my weight on the couch the TV picture became severely distorted. I had total control. I didn't fight anymore. "Go ahead, sister dearest, watch your show." I'd make a slight motion on the couch, and she'd run up to adjust the television set. No sooner did she return to the couch than I would cause the picture to scramble again. I would suggest that maybe God didn't want her to annoy her brother so much and was punishing her with the "picture-tube plague." She would run to Mother, insisting that I was the cause. I suggested that she live a more pious life and not invoke God's wrath. I suggested that the best way for her to start would be to show compassion for her brother.

My sister complained, "Mom, I know he's doing it."

"Mom, I'm blamed for everything that goes wrong," I insisted, sitting there angelically.

"Can't you see your brother is just sitting there? He's not doing anything. Stop picking on him!" my mother would counter.

Finally my sister would run out in frustration, and I got to watch my show.

There was one television show that my sister and I agreed upon, and that was "Mr. and Mrs. North," a spy mystery show. My sister and I would huddle together if the scenes got scary enough.

Each of us knew that the other was capable of being totally terrified, and how to bring it about. In Yiddish the word for "going" is the same as the word for "ghost." After watching a scary show that my sister knew was particularly frightening for me, she'd exit the room, and in a slow, eerie and ghostly manner would say, "Are you going? Are you going?" meaning "The ghost. The ghost."

I would yell to no avail, "Mom, she's trying to scare me!"

My sister retorted, "No such thing, I just asked him if he's coming." Five minutes later, she would do it again.

One night, I decided to let my sister have it. After watching an Alfred Hitchcock episode, she started to settle down to go to sleep. I announced to all that I was going outside to the corner candy store to be with my friends. I made sure she heard the announcement and saw me leave the apartment and lock the door. Once outside, I ran around the building, climbed the one and a half stories to her window, let myself in and hid under her bed. There I waited. At last she came in, shut the light and lay down on her bed. I still had to wait and be very quiet. I wanted her to be groggy and almost asleep.

When the motion of her bed subsided, I knew the time was right. I raised my legs and arms to different quadrants of the mattress and began in turn to apply pressure slowly in different places. I kept at it while making the faintest ghost sounds. I felt her grab onto the mattress and gasp in a most horrified manner. I applied more pressure, and increased the ghost sounds. She held on a few seconds more, then darted to my parents' bedroom, screaming at the top of her lungs.

My sister demanded swift and severe punishment. My parents put on a real show of anger and yelled at me, but I caught my father giggling in the corner, and I knew I was safe. My sister kept protesting. I was punished finally, but it was worth it. I'd do it again.

Escape from the City
(1956 - age 16)

Summers in Brooklyn were steamy and humid. We fried in the bitter heat and suffocated from the moisture hanging in the air and around our necks. Our ten-inch electric fan gave some relief, but only if you sat directly in front of it. Going to camp was out of the question. Who could afford camp? Being a counselor was my only hope.

It was early spring, and the newspapers were full of summer camp advertisements. Perfect. They needed campers, I needed to be a counselor. I wrote to some of those camps for informational brochures. Looking at these brochures was in itself an escape for me. Look at those lakes, the water skiing, archery, arts and crafts! I've got to become a camp counselor.

But who would take me? Archery? No, never got near a bow and arrow. Water skiing? Who was I kidding? It looked as if to be hired as a counselor, you needed to have years of experience as a camper.

Now here's a little camp. Look - it has a lake. I'll tell them what a good swimmer I am. I'll tell them I know arts and crafts, and then I'll figure out what to do once I see what's in the arts and crafts shack. After all, I am very handy! That's it, I'll tell them that besides being a counselor par excellence, I'm also very handy. If anything in the camp should break down, I'll fix it. No, that's not enough. It says here to write about the activities you are proficient in. Look at how much space they supply under this question! I can't leave it blank. Hey - look at this brochure of a camp in Vermont. It doesn't have horses. Nope, nowhere do they mention horses. The other camps mention horses. If they had horses, I'm sure they would mention it too. I'll tell them what an excellent equestrian I am. Since they don't have horses, they'll never be the wiser, and my application will seem more complete. They'll think I know something about something.

During my interview I bluffed about my past experiences. I told them I had been to camps in Europe. I didn't mention that they were DP camps. Then I asked the owner about his horses. "Exactly how many horses do you have? Oh, that's too bad. Yes, that's right, you don't have horses. It is by far my greatest strength, but you don't have any. Oh well, what can you do."

Off to Vermont. On the way, the camp owner picked me up as well as four of the campers who also lived in New York. The camp was a very exclusive one, with less than two dozen well-bred children of diplomats. Their ages varied from six to twelve. The total counselor staff consisted of two college coeds and myself. The three of us would split the children up into different activity groups.

It was a very good summer for me. I learned water skiing, archery, different ball games, and all the other activities peculiar to camps. Every time I had to lead an activity I knew nothing about, I simply asked which camper wanted to volunteer to demonstrate to the others how the activity was performed. I asked them to demonstrate in such a way that even someone who had never done it before could follow. There was never a shortage of volunteers. These kids knew everything ad boredom. I think these little diplomats went to camp from the time they were six months old.

The camp owner developed a great trust in me, probably as a result of my ability to repair things.

He taught me how to drive almost immediately, and as the activities were scattered throughout the camp grounds, he let me pack the car with kids and drive them from one activity to another.

One day, my little white lie came back to haunt me. The owner announced how pleased he was with things and since we had a fine equestrian among us, he had entered into a contract with the stable up the road. Starting the following week the kids would be able to go riding with me. With me?

The other two counselors weren't much help since they weren't thrilled about horses. The only advice they could offer me was that horses were big and sometimes kicked.

Needless to say, I myself was afraid of horses. In anticipation, I went to town and picked up a book about horses. I read it over a few times and felt somewhat prepared. I was still petrified, mind you, but tried not to let on. "Which one of you has ridden a horse before?" Thank God they all raised their hands. "Okay, who wants to demonstrate the safety aspects of horseback riding?" They all raised their hands again. In this way I learned the fundamentals of riding.

How macho I felt. It was wonderful to be on top of a horse and feel the power. We were one, the horse and I. Together we were so strong. Perhaps the horse contributed a little more to the strength formula. No matter. It wasn't the horse that I wanted to ride. It was Alicia.

Alicia was also a counselor at this camp. She was Scandinavian. She was only two years older than I, but she was a woman. I just knew it. The other counselor, Susan, was also Alicia's age. They both acted like older sisters towards me. I hated that. Susan actually came over to my bed one night, tucked me in, and gave me a goodnight kiss right on my lips.

I wasn't sure what that meant. I didn't know if she was truly innocent and didn't realize what she was doing to my hormones, or if this was a game to tease me to death. I found them both attractive, but it was Alicia that I really wanted. Besides, Alicia seemed more promising. Susan was American, whereas Alicia was also European, although much more Americanized than I. Still, we had fewer cultural differences. Susan used to sings songs like "Nobody likes me, everybody hates me, I'm gonna eat some worms." All the campers seemed to know that song, too. Alicia and I were the only two who didn't know it. We had ignorance in common.

One starlit evening after the children were put to bed, Alicia and I took a walk. As we made light chatter about the day's activities, I suddenly turned and kissed her. Before I knew what was happening we were rolling in the hay, locked in each other's embrace. I couldn't believe it. She'd been waiting for me to touch her. She was an explosion just waiting to happen. Susan tucked me in and made me wonder, but Alicia had never given me a single clue.

In moments my hands were inside her bra. We were kissing and touching under the stars, with enough light to see each other's expressions and enough darkness to feel safe from being observed. We couldn't have been farther than one hundred feet from the main house.

Her blouse was now totally open, her brassiere had been removed, and she wasn't resisting. I dared to open her dungaree zipper and put my hand in. First I touched her thighs, but soon I was bold enough to pet her all over. There was hay under and all around us. It was hot and wonderful. I didn't dare put my hands inside her panties yet. This was all going a little too fast. I wasn't sure she would let me go that far. I wanted to pull down her dungarees completely to rub against her better, but her pants were tight, and there were constant noises from the main house. What if the owners come out, or turn on the flood lights? Alicia would never be able to compose herself in time with her pants off. God, why did I pick such a lousy spot? Well, how was I to know? I had no idea I would get this far. I had no idea I would get anywhere. Why couldn't she have worn a skirt? Yes, a loose skirt with no underwear. Maybe we can move to another place? No, once she puts her bra on she may not take it off again. I'm staying here.

We kept kissing and touching. She even complimented me for being so experienced. Alicia was much more developed and mature than I. She recognized my inexperience immediately and was bright and sensitive enough to build up my ego. When she told me that she could tell I was experienced, well, at that moment I felt like there wasn't a horse so big that I couldn't mount it.

The next day we both behaved as if nothing had happened. I suppose for her, nothing did happen. But for me it was everything. I never got a second opportunity to be with her. She was a woman, she needed more. I was still a boy.

Turning Point: Lowell and Physics
(1956 - age 16 1/2)

By the time I was sixteen I spoke English well, and had read one complete book - Tom Sawyer. I could understand much of what was on television except for comedy and idioms. And I still couldn't understand a word the disc jockeys said on the radio.

My parents were struggling financially, but they now had their own business, a women's clothing store in the marketplace near our house.

It was clear to me that I had no future of any kind. My parents pressed me to help them out in the store, hoping I would develop an interest in becoming a storekeeper. I wanted to do something different with my life. I lost interest in the noisy marketplace, with the merchants loudly hawking their wares and pulling people over to make a sale. Not much different than the way it was in Azerbaijan.

There was one aspect of selling woman's clothing, however, that I did not mind. When a woman tried on a skirt, my father would insert two fingers at the waistband. If the fingers fit, it meant the skirt was too large and a smaller size was needed. Whenever I did help out, I would wait for an attractive woman to enter and eagerly offer to help fit her with a skirt. "Miss, are you sure you don't need a new skirt to go with that new handkerchief you're buying?"

One day moving trucks came to my building, and with them arrived Lowell. I watched to see what interesting belongings might move into our building with Lowell. It turned out that most of what moved in with Lowell was books. The books seemed heavier than he did. Lowell was small for his age, and young for his grade.

Lowell and I became friends. We did not become close friends. It was more of an alliance. Lowell was two years younger than I but was already in his junior year in high school, the same as I. He had skipped grades twice.

I hung around Lowell because I liked him and was in total awe of his academic prowess. Imagine, he had read Moby Dick. From the size of it, it would surely take me a year to read. Lowell probably hung around with me because I was an interesting oddity. I thought of him as a knower and he probably saw me as a doer. I venture to guess that the only thing Lowell didn't know was how I could do anything without knowing a thing.

One day Lowell and I planned to have lunch together. I was to meet him at his last class prior to the lunch period. I arrived a little early. The door to his classroom had a glass window in it, and I peeked inside.

A class full of Lowells! No, they weren't all small, but there was a sameness in their mannerisms and intent posture. They all listened attentively. The teacher never had to yell at them to be quiet. In fact, it seemed almost as if the teacher whispered, and the students were intent on not missing one word. This was not at all like my classrooms. All the kids had slide rules either on their desk or swinging from their hips, and many of them also had T-squares. The blackboard looked most interesting, too. It was filled with graphs, curves, equations, sine waves and Greek letters. On the teacher's desk sat a cyclotron with arcs of electricity flying across the table like in Frankenstein movies.

At lunch I asked Lowell what class he was in.

"Physics," he replied.

"What is physics?" I asked. He handed me the textbook. I leafed through it. The book had pictures of optical gadgets, light being reflected through lenses, pulleys, electric circuits and so many other fascinating things. This was the kind of stuff I needed!

I dashed to the student advisor and presented my demand to take this course in the second half of my junior year. The advisor had an answer immediately. "Impossible."

"It's what I really want," I explained.

But it was really, really impossible, she insisted. Her explanation was that the kids taking physics were not only enrolled in the academic program, but were also honor students. She emphasized that many of them would avoid physics altogether if they could, because it was considered a very difficult subject. Furthermore, there was the requirement that students, as a prerequisite, needed to have completed one year of algebra, one year of geometry, and take trigonometry as a co-requisite. Without that background there would be no hope of passing physics.

She reminded me that unlike the classes I was taking, this was an academic course and did not come with an automatic passing grade. Then she reminded me that my grades to date were all just minimum passing grades, and that failing physics would jeopardize my graduating and receiving a general diploma. I insisted that I didn't care about the general diploma. My classes were disgustingly boring. I begged her to let me take physics. She responded, "Absolutely not."

"Fine." I said. "Then I'm not coming back to school." and I started walking out. As I left she reminded me that school was compulsory. I shot back, "Check my homeroom tomorrow. You won't see me there."

The next day I was summoned to appear with my parents. I sat in front of my advisor with my mother. My mother could hardly understand English, let alone comprehend the situation at hand. The advisor asked me to translate for my mother.

I explained, "Mother, the advisor asked me to tell you that I threatened not to return to school if I cannot take the course I want." In turn I told the grade advisor, "My mother said that I am very strong-willed, and that if I said I won't go to school, you can depend on it."

The advisor immediately understood that she was not going to make much progress with my mother and tried a different approach. "Let's make a deal," she said. "Take algebra. If you just pass one semester of algebra, I will let you take physics the following semester (senior year). Just pass algebra."

"What is algebra?" I asked. She pulled out a book and I flipped through the pages. It didn't captivate me as much as the physics book had, but it still looked a lot more intriguing than the general math I was taking. The prospect of not having to learn about percentages one more time was in itself sufficient. "I agree," I said, realizing that this was the best I could bargain for.

The algebra class was full of Lowell types too. They were all younger than I. They all listened to the teacher. They did not throw chalk or erasers at each other or at the teacher. This was so refreshing, so different from anything I had experienced in my other classes. I made new friends, little scholastic types who planned their lives out. I loved the class. I loved the teacher. I did the homework. I loved algebra. And most of all, I loved doing well. I got an A.

When the semester was over, I again went to see my advisor. She exclaimed, "I don't understand it, but I know you didn't cheat, because I understand you got the highest test scores in the class. Very well. I'll keep my promise. You can take Algebra II and Physics I in the fall."

"No," I said, "I want that, but now I also want my other courses to be switched over to the academic program."

She pointed out that I would not get an academic diploma regardless. I responded that it was not the diploma I cared about, it was the courses that were important. The discussion ended. I got what I wanted.

My senior year was a good year. I started getting A's and B's in many of my courses, including an A in physics. I had a new group of friends. I graduated with the general diploma, but with a new perspective on the possibilities for my life, even if those possibilities were still quite remote.

New Name
(1958 - age 18)

My new friends were refreshingly different, more interesting. Even their names seemed more interesting. I decided that I needed a better name. I didn't think Joe was a suitable name for me anymore. I needed a new name to better fit the new me, the me that might possibly be a good student, the me that might possibly be somebody someday.

So, Lowell and a few of my other new friends went through the telephone book with me, searching for a more appropriate name. We took a vote and officially dubbed me "Elliot."

My parents took the name change in stride. They only spoke Yiddish and only called me by my Yiddish name anyway, so this didn't represent much of a change for them. If someone telephoned me, however, they'd ask, "Who? Oh yes, Elliot. Wait a minute." My new English name was too hard to pronounce. It's not that they minded the name change. They just kept asking me why I had to choose such an abnormal one.

This was a very important event. It was more than just a name change. It was the beginning of a total makeover. I wasn't going to be a "Joe" as in Joe's Bar & Grill. I was going to be more of an "Elliot," as in T.S. Eliot. My name change was simply in anticipation, like an announcement to the world of my forthcoming change. How would it sound anyway, "Professor Joe"?

College

(1958 - age 18)

Now that I had a taste of it, I hungered for an education. I'd seen both sides now, the hoods and the Lowells, and I was sure which side was better.

I wanted to go to college. Going to an out-of-town college was strictly beyond the family's means, so my applications went to the local schools. It was 1958, and the requirements were very rigid. New York City had many schools, but they were all very competitive. The city colleges, being free, had fierce competition for their engineering programs. I applied to every local school, including the junior colleges, even though they didn't offer engineering programs.

By this time I could express myself reasonably well. I sent the colleges a cover letter explaining my special circumstances and hopefully justifying my earlier performance, or lack of it. I pointed to my last year's achievement as an indication of my potential.

They all gave me the benefit of early decision. In an unexpectedly short time I was rejected by every single school, including the community colleges. In one case I even received a letter from the admissions officer insulting me for applying.

With that door closed to me, I went to work. The job entailed opening envelopes for a vitamin company and separating the money from the coupons. These envelopes often contained complaints from elderly users who were upset that the vitamins did not enhance their sex lives as promised.

I went to my boss with one of these letters in defense of one ninety-five year old. I felt we should send this man his money back. I explained to the boss that the man had taken the vitamins and still couldn't do it.

"Can he put the money in the envelope and lick it?" my boss asked.

"Yes," I responded.

To which the boss replied, "Then he can do it!"

"But that's not what the man wants to do," I protested.

"But that's what we want him to do," he responded.

This was my introduction to industry. I had been on the job for six months when I received a phone call. The call was from Brooklyn Community College. A seat had become available and, if I still had an interest, they would take me on probation, even though my achievements fell way short of their minimum admission requirements.

The qualified invitation was good enough for me. I dropped the job and enrolled in the January semester, in a program leading to an associate degree in construction technology. It was a new experience for me to be a star pupil. I was learning so much, and loving it.

After I completed the first year, with top grades, I knew that I had a chance to transfer to a four-year college. I started to set my sights on a career in engineering. I applied to some of the better schools in the city. This time I pointed to my grades at the community college as an indication of possible potential.

Virtually all the schools accepted me on the condition that I receive no credit for the work I did at the community college, and that I enter as a freshman, again on probation. I felt the risk was too great. By now, I knew something about the kids enrolled in engineering schools. They were tough cookies. I'd be competing with kids who came from Bronx High School of Science, Brooklyn Tech, Stuyvesant. These kids were not only smart, they were well-prepared. Many of them had already taken calculus in high school. Being top student at the community college assured me that I would graduate and have an associate degree. On the other hand, if I transferred at this point and fell on my face, I wouldn't even have a respectable high school diploma to fall back on. I passed on the opportunity and remained at the junior college for a second year.

After graduating from junior college, I again applied to the four-year colleges that had previously accepted me, fearing, however, that I had angered them by declining their prior offers of admission. Once again they all accepted me, with the same condition that I enter as a freshman on probation. I had applied to the engineering program at every college but one. Columbia University had just started a new program. This program was a joint effort involving their departments of engineering, law, and business. It was called Construction Management.

I opted for Columbia University. I feared the engineering curriculum could be too difficult, too risky for me. I judged I had a greater chance of succeeding in the construction management program. Another reason I opted for Columbia was that I didn't have a respectable high school diploma. A degree from Columbia was a sure way to overcome all the negative status from my past, and to reaffirm to the world and to myself that I was not a cut below.

As the semester progressed I realized three things. First, that I was capable of handling the academic work at Columbia. Second, if I transferred into the engineering curriculum, I could probably handle that, too. Third, that the two-hour commute each way to school would kill me for sure.

Tuition was a strain on the family, so living on campus was completely out of the question. I had always kept a part-time job for spending money, but it was not enough to even think of renting an apartment near campus.

Alas, I saw a notice on the campus bulletin board. "Spending money plus free room and board one block from campus, in exchange for some light typing, and chauffeuring a distinguished lady around a few hours a week." Perfect, I thought. Remember,

I took wood shop, metal shop, and did I forget to mention typing classes?

I rushed to meet the woman who had placed the ad, with great certainty that this job was in my pocket. She was an apparently successful psychiatrist confined to a wheelchair. As we discussed the job duties, it became painfully clear that she was looking for more than a boarder. So I reluctantly passed up my only opportunity to live near the university campus.

For the following semester, the fall of 1961, I transferred to the engineering department at Pratt Institute. Pratt Institute is in Brooklyn, and was much closer to my home. My acceptance was also on condition that I start as a freshman, and, furthermore, that I would have to complete a year of geometry, intermediate algebra, trigonometry and advanced algebra before I started. I took all of the above in the summer prior to the fall semester so that I was now prepared to start with calculus, as a freshman at Pratt at the age of twenty-one.

What I really wanted to major in was architecture, but the fear of starving as an architect haunted me. My insecurities were still too great. I already understood that success in the field of architecture was very dependent upon getting commissions. Who in the world was going to give me a commission to design anything? Who would even offer to let me design an addition to their home? I didn't know anybody who even owned a home. What about serious commissions? Would the Kennedys drive down my street in Brooklyn? I could just hear one of the them saying to the other, "Here, pull over. As long as we're in this Brooklyn neighborhood, let's ring the bell of this architect Elliot Rais." Or perhaps I would meet some celebrities at a party. I know I'm not on the invitation list, but I could crash and say I'm on the bride's side.

No, I decided I had better study engineering. It was safer, and my ticket out of the slums.

More often than not I audited an evening high school course at the same time I was taking an advanced version of it at college. For instance, not having had chemistry in high school, I lacked the background for my physical chemistry course in college. So I attended an evening high school chemistry course as often as I could, to fill in the holes in my education. The holes in my background notwithstanding, I emerged as a fine student. As time went on, I acquired a greater reservoir of knowledge and my studies became easier for me.

First Love
(1961 - age 21)

Imet Patricia at a freshman dance at Pratt. She was an art student, sporting culottes and long black hair. She smiled at me, a smile that stretched from ear to ear. She was from upstate, and her soft mannerisms overwhelmed me.

Patricia became my first real girlfriend. Patricia and I were hot, but we had virtually no opportunity to fulfill our desires. She lived in a dormitory and in those days, dorms were strictly segregated. My parents knew that I was seeing a Catholic girl and didn't want her in their home. In fact, they didn't even want to hear about her.

Somehow, they always knew if a girl I was seeing wasn't Jewish. They had antennae for such things.

"See you later, Mom."

"Where are you going?"

"To the movies."

"Alone?"

"No, with a friend."

"A friend without a name?"

"No, Mom. She has a name."

"So what's her name?"

"Patricia."

"What kind of Jewish name is Patricia?"

At that point, she would start yelling. She would ask me if I thought that the short hairs on shiksas grew in a different direction - in other words, did I think they were better in bed? Or something like that.

Patricia and I were desperate for any opportunity for sexual intimacy. Since I knew my parents' schedule, sometimes I would risk bringing Patricia to our house. This was chancy, and tense. Because their store was so close to the house, I could never be sure that my parents wouldn't just drop in unexpectedly.

I was already gun-shy. This had, in fact, happened, about a year earlier. My parents came home while I was in bed with a girl. She and I were both completely naked, and the mystery of sex was about to unfold. It had taken a long time, but finally here I was, in bed with a beautiful girl. I didn't have a cast on my leg this time and I didn't have to be a mere consultant. I was finally going to experience sex myself.

I had forgotten all about my parents. Until I heard the sound of keys jingling ...

"Oh my God!" I yelled. "It's my parents!" I had locked the apartment door from the inside, so I had to go open it. I started getting dressed and threw my guitar at the girl. I hoped maybe we could present an innocent tableau, me and this girl, just sitting around singing and playing the guitar.

I ran toward the door to open it, but then turned and ran back to make sure my guest was composed.

There she was, sitting and playing the guitar - completely naked. Shock and fear had rendered her helpless.

I stalled my parents for a few more minutes as I helped her get dressed. My parents weren't dumb. That girl never came to our home again. Sex would remain a mystery for a while longer.

Back to Patricia. As naive as I still was about sex, Patricia seemed even more so. I couldn't understand this. I figured her sexual organ was the more complex one - why didn't she know everything? A man's organ is self-revealing. You take one look and you can see it all; not too much to figure out.

I did bring Patricia home a few times. In those brief, tense moments, we both tried, but we were so timid and nervous that we kept looking at the door at the slightest sound. We never managed to pull it off, at least not there.

It might have happened on one occasion, in the back seat of someone's car. To this day, I'm not sure.

Patricia, however, assured me that it had happened. In fact, two months later she told me she was pregnant.

Pregnant? This was terrible. How could it be? After all, we hardly... Or had we? (I'm still not sure.) Well, I'd just have to marry her. It was a terrible thing and the timing was worse. But... I did love her.

Enter my parents. Marry her? Had I lost my mind? Not only would they throw me out of the house, but they were going to say the prayer for the dead and disown me.

They insisted that the best thing to do was to arrange for an abortion. Abortions were illegal. How could they suggest that I send my dear Patricia to some butcher in some alleyway? No, no, they would round up the money for a trip to Puerto Rico. The procedure would be performed in a hospital, legally and safely.

The pressure was great. I succumbed. I gave Patricia the money, wrapped in my tears, and told her it was the only way. I could not defy both my family and my circumstances. If I left school at that point, we would have no future.

Patricia took the money. A week later, she returned it. She told me she'd only been testing me, to see if I could break away from my family for her. Her fears had been well-founded.

Patricia was graceful and forbidden, as the church in Germany had been. I loved her, but the bonds of the past and my need for security made the outcome inevitable. It was over.

Mexico
(1962 - age 22, Sophomore at Pratt Institute)

In 1962 a distant young cousin from Mexico was passing through the States. She stayed with us in Brooklyn, and a flirtatious friendship developed. This led to letter-writing and ultimately a campaign by her for me to visit Mexico. She mailed me brochures from Mexico City College, and pointed out that with the low value of the peso, I could spend the summer in Mexico City for about the same cost as tuition for summer school in New York. The plan was seductive.

Pratt Institute was not interested in accepting credit for any course work I did in Mexico, pointing to the differences in academic standards. But I persisted and persuaded the registrar that what I would forego academically would be compensated for by the cultural experience, so long as I didn't take any serious courses there, such as math or thermodynamics. A deal was struck whereby I was allowed to fulfill some humanity requirements by taking literature and philosophy.

After three days and nights on a bus from New York, I arrived in Mexico City to be greeted by my cousin and her family. They pressed me to live with them. This was not my plan, however. I had been assigned to a Mexican family by the university. But my cousins wouldn't hear of it. They insisted I honor them by at least staying with them the two weeks before my classes started. During my stay with them they arranged dates or social engagements for me with their daughter practically every night. I felt very pressured and couldn't wait to get out.

When classes started I moved out of my cousins' house and in with a university-referred Mexican family. These families welcomed American students, partially for the money but mostly because they had children and wanted the cultural exchange, particularly the practice of English.

My Mexican relatives were angered, and they wrote to my family to advise them what a no-good bum I was. Apparently I had caused them some loss of face in their community. After all, a party had been held in my honor when I arrived, and apparently unbeknownst to me, expectations regarding me and their daughter were high. Mexican social customs surrounding these matters were different.

On the first day of class, I met Cathy. Beautiful, blond California liberal Cathy. It was love at first sight. No, no, it can't be love. I'm not getting involved with another gentile. I had tried it and had already learned that I did not want the prayer for the dead recited over me.

The mutual attraction, however, was great. I told Cathy my story and explained that even though philosophically I was an agnostic, as a matter of practicality I was a Jewish agnostic, if one could be such a thing, and that I was very likely destined to marry a Jewish girl someday. Cathy rebutted that she had not proposed marriage. She asked if we couldn't just take it easy and enjoy the summer? It did not take much persuading. It was the best summer of my life. Palm trees, mariachis, and Cathy.

By the time the summer had ended, Cathy and I had long since forgotten our covenant for a limited involvement and were in a loving relationship. I kissed her at the airport, and she promised to write every day. I knew Cathy to be a prolific writer from the long letters she wrote to me almost daily when we lived only a few kilometers apart in Mexico. My writing at that time was very strained, but I promised to respond as best I could.

I arrived back in Brooklyn after a whole summer's absence and a three-day bus journey to a scene I hadn't expected. My parents immediately attacked me, yelling furiously. My mother chased me with a rolling pin and actually swung it at me.

"What is it?" I demanded. "I can't understand what you're saying if you're chasing me and screaming!"

My mother kept chasing, swinging, and screaming, "You chigali! We didn't raise you to be a chigali!"

"Mom, what's a chigali?"

After everyone calmed down, I discovered what this was all about. One time, while I was in Mexico City, Cathy had invited me to go to Acapulco. I had already been to Acapulco the week before I met her, so I resisted. But Carol and her roommate came over to my place to persuade me. They were both going, and wanted my company. I cited the reading homework I had to do, the fact that I had just been there with my cousin, and the expense. They responded that this time, with the two of them along, it would be much more fun. Besides, Mexico was not a place for ladies to travel unescorted, and what's more, money was no object to them. They had decided to jointly treat me to the trip. Yes, they would pay for the trip. They were both quite wealthy, and this was a trivial expense to both of them. I yielded. (But I did pay my own way.) This whole discussion took place in the living room of the Mexican family with whom I was staying.

What I didn't know was that my outraged Mexican relatives were keeping careful tabs on what I was doing. My activities were recounted in letters to my parents. One such letter told my parents about the life I was leading. It described my existence as a "gigolo," detailing my trip to Acapulco with two shiksas, who paid to take me along in order to have sex orgies. Thus, I certainly was a "gigolo". My parents' pronunciation of gigolo was "chigali."

So much for the gigolo incident.

I never got a single letter from Cathy after I returned. I was hurt, disillusioned and sad. Once more I felt the pain of losing a love. This time there was also the sexual bonding. I had felt so whole with her, the woman with whom I had achieved my sense of manhood. All that was left were my memories of Mexico with palm trees, mangos, mariachis and Cathy... and making love with Cathy in a hot room in Acapulco with a ceiling fan evaporating the beads of our perspiration... while the sun fought through the cracks of the louvers to remind us it was the middle of the day.

I missed her. I thought of her in the morning and at night and I would hide and cry. How could she not write! Is this the way it is with liberal shiksas raised in Scarsdale? She slept with me the first night we met and loved me all summer and now that she's back at UCLA did she already have her next lover for the new semester? I was furious, and loved her, and hated her for abandoning me.

It wasn't until years later, when I was almost twenty-seven years old, and a few weeks before my own marriage, that I heard from Cathy again. Imagine my surprise when she told me she was in New York and could see me the next day at her hotel! I couldn't sleep. I kept thinking of how she would look when I saw her. I kept seeing her in bed, and feeling so guilty about it. That was, after all, forbidden. I was getting married soon. I wondered what she was doing here, was she married, what the hell does she want to see me now for? No! I'm not going to see that bitch - she has some nerve. But I had to see her. I had to find out what had happened.

I went to her hotel room. We embraced and immediately she asked why I hadn't answered any of her letters. "Cathy," I said, "I wrote to you and waited forever, and never received anything from you."

She told me that she had written a letter each day for months, and that she had telephoned and left messages for me.

"Impossible," I said.

"Ask your parents. They probably threw them out."

I didn't want to believe that. But then again, I also couldn't believe that she had abandoned me.

At home I confronted my mother about the letters. She hesitated, then went over to a closet, pulled out a few boxes of letters, and threw them at me. "Here, go to your shiksa!" she proclaimed.

I blew up with rage. I screamed at my parents until my voice gave. I was disappointed at my parents for going beyond what I had imagined they were capable of. I was disappointed in myself for not trusting in Cathy's love and taking more drastic measures to pursue her.

It was too late. I was getting married. She was on her way to Africa to meet her boyfriend and pursue some academic project. Cathy was the past. We had different lives now.

Skiing
(1962 - age 22)

During my college years I learned about sports. Some, like tennis, I could afford. Others, like skiing, were prohibitively expensive. When I discovered skiing, I thought it was the best thing in the world. From my experience as a summer camp counselor, I had learned to be comfortable with sports. By this time I could water-ski and ice skate fairly well, so snow skiing was an adaptation of previous skills that I already had under control.

But with my budget, I could afford to do it only once a year. This was not enough. I wanted more than anything to ski.

One day I saw an ad in a local paper soliciting ski instructors. Those hired for the job would first be instructed in a uniform training method prior to the season. Then, during the ski season, the employers promised weekend trips to the mountains, where we would teach a little in the mornings, then ski to our hearts' content the rest of the day. On top of this they also provided a little spending money. This job was definitely for me, if only I could get it.

On the designated evening I went down for an interview, undaunted by the fact that I had only skied twice in my life. In the ski shop were a hundred other aspiring ski instructors. They were dressed in the latest regalia and spoke to each other in "ski-zen-eeze." I wore dungarees and a shirt. Perhaps I can pass as understated? In turn the owners of the ski school addressed each person in the crowd, with everyone else able to hear the conversation.

"You, how long have you skied?"

"Twelve years."

"Where have you skied?"

"Mount Snow, Killington."

"Do you know Hans there at Killington?"

"Yes, yes I helped him out in the ski school last year."

"Okay, you're in. You over there, where have you skied?"

And so it went. I noticed that the ones who skied the most, the farthest, and/or wore the fanciest outfits got in, while the others were sent home. I had never even heard of Killington, nor did I know any Hans. I knew I was in deep trouble. I haven't got a chance here, I thought.

"You, there, in the dungarees." Oops, that's me. "I suppose you have a lot of skiing under your belt, too, huh?" (with a chuckle). Here it goes.

"Yah," I said, with a heavy, artificial German accent. By this time, I could speak English quite well. On the other hand, there was hardly any accent I could not imitate to a T. I had been surrounded by accents my whole life, and I used to have quite a bit of fun imitating them. Besides, I had taken German at Columbia University.

"Yah, I have skied very much."

"How many years have you skied?"

"I don't remember," I said, "since age three or four."

"Where have you skied?"

"Ins my backyard, yah."

"And where might that backyard be?"

"Where I wast born, in Switzerland. Yah, furst I learned to ski und then to walk, yah."

"Okay, you're in."

For a few weeks we were taught a uniform teaching method in the ski shop. We had a text and some xeroxed sheets describing how to teach every maneuver - the herringbone, sidestep, how to get up, stem christie, full christie. It was all there in the notes. I studied hard, and on the wooden floor of the ski shop I could ski with the best of them.

The last three weekends before the season we were taken to Hunter Mountain. We went through our routine, showing how we would teach certain things and what to emphasize, what the pitfalls were, and what the beginners were likely to do wrong. I did all of this for two hours each morning. Then it was free time for the instructors to ski and play. At this point I carefully disappeared and found a remote hill where I wouldn't be seen, to try out these maneuvers. I practiced until I was black and blue. By the end of the winter I was a decent skier.

The success of wiggling into the ski instructor's position helped raise my self-esteem. More and more I began to see myself as one capable of doing most anything I put my mind to. On the other hand, this new exposure and contact with a lifestyle I had seen only in movies as a child in DP camp now made me envious.

When I saw such a lifestyle in the movies, as a child, or even as a teenager in Brooklyn, it had little effect on me. It had no relevance to me. Now I had touched it. It could have something to do with me. Another way of life began to appear attainable, but I could not yet have it. In the DP camp, very little was attainable. There was a distant hope, like the hope of winning a lottery. But I don't think there was much frustration. We had very little, but no one expected or felt entitled to much more. It was out of our realm. Here, almost everything seemed attainable. Here, it was all around us. If you didn't have something, it almost felt like you were the only one who still didn't have it. This was the American frustration.

Tango
(1962 - age 22)

As a student, I always needed extra money. My typing skill was helpful. I was able to pick up various typing jobs, and also became a part-time keypunch operator. But this money was never enough.

When a dance studio ran an advertisement looking for dance instructors, I applied. By that time, I could dance quite well, and I thought that this would be a fun way to earn extra cash. I also had the illusion of meeting attractive girls.

The studio hired me, and then trained me in their teaching method. The learning part was fun, but my illusions quickly faded. The students were older, overweight women who were only too happy to hang all over me and hold me in a death grip while I tried to teach them the intimate tango.

I realized that the studio was taking money from these lonely women so that they could play out their sexual fantasies at my expense. Was I really becoming a gigolo with the title of Dance Instructor? I could hear my mother whispering, "Chigali - you're a Chigali." Professor Chigali? The vitamins I sold didn't turn men into Don Juans, and these studios weren't turning out Ginger Rogerses. Was this what the business world was really all about? I left the studio wondering how this could be.

Saving Face
(1964 - age 24)

W hen I went off to college, I totally lost track of Lowell. He went off to Brooklyn College and I haven't seen him since. The only friend I had and still have from the past is Jerry. That is, when he is a friend. What I mean is, well, there is a deep affection between us, but Jerry is at his peak when I'm in total agony. This is what I mean.

Jerry was sort of a Lowell type. He was a year older than I to start with, and between his accelerated classes and my slow start, Jerry was already gainfully employed by the time I entered Pratt Institute.

On one occasion we went on a double date. It was a really important date for each of us. I skimmed from my allowance money for weeks, to buy tickets to Goethe's Faust at City Center. I must have really wanted to impress this girl.

We went to City Center and saw the opera. Now it was time to have a bite. It hadn't occurred to me to discuss these details with Jerry in advance. I suggested we head straight up to Columbia University to the Lion's Den. With my (expired) Columbia University student card, we could spend a couple of hours there and have a cheeseburger and beverage at prices I was prepared for.

"No," said Jerry. He had a better idea. He suggested another place a bit closer.

"Jerry," I whispered, "You know I can't afford a city restaurant."

"Trust me," Jerry assured me. "It's all right."

Now Jerry and I had somewhat different circumstances. He was a professional programmer while I was existing on a meager allowance plus what I could earn doing miscellaneous part-time jobs.

We arrived at Davey Jones Seafood Locker. I noticed the fashionably dressed maitre'd, those chairs, those tablecloths.

"Jerry," I whispered, "did you lose your mind? This place will cost a fortune! I'm broke! I'm still paying off these tickets!"

"Don't worry," he whispered, "I'll lend you the money."

"I don't want to borrow any more, Jerry. I'll be paying it off for the next six months!"

"Then just order something inexpensive, Elliot. Besides, it's too late. We can't leave now."

When I saw the menu, I wanted to kill Jerry. The place was outrageous for my budget! There was absolutely nothing on that menu that I could afford. Well, I'm on an important date and can't let on, so I've got to make the best of it.

My date was suitably impressed and made the reasonable assumption that since we had brought them to this place, we could afford it. So she ordered lobster, with all the trimmings of course. I was beside myself. I'm wrong, I thought, I won't be paying this off for six months - more like six years!

In desperation to somehow offset this disastrous bill, I studied the right side of the menu carefully. The only items not totally prohibitive were the raw oysters. I had seen these things in clam bars on the way to Rockaway Beach but I could never understand how anybody could actually eat them. Never mind that these were non-kosher, because intellectually I was relatively liberated. On the other hand, these things were major non-kosher, not to mention slimy and disgusting. The only food I ever ate had been overcooked for hours. Never had I eaten anything raw (except for the bugs in Russia, that is, and they weren't slimy).

The waiter took everyone's order and then stood next to me. "And you, sir," he said.

"I shall have these oysters over here." I pointed to the item on the menu so that he wouldn't confuse them with the more expensive oysters further down.

"But that, sir, is an appetizer," he pointed out.

"Oh, yes, I'm very well aware of that," I said, "but I love these raw oysters and shall have them as a main course."

"Very well, sir," he responded. Secretly, I was hoping that he wouldn't be satisfied with my order and would ask us all to leave, but that didn't happen.

The food arrived, and everyone was preoccupied examining their plates. Everyone, that is, except Jerry. Jerry was busy examining my face. After I looked at my dish, I looked over at him. Jerry had the ability to keep a straight face and make his eyes smile. His eyes weren't laughing at me, just smiling, as if to say, "I'm kind of sorry about this, Elliot, but boy, am I going to enjoy watching you eat those!" I knew what his eyes were saying, and he knew I knew, and I knew he knew that I knew. I really wanted to cut his throat for this, and I also knew that he knew that.

"Would you like some sauce with this, sir?"

"Oh yes, that's how I especially love it." I drenched those wiggling, slimy little suckers in the red sauce. I discreetly pierced them with my fork a few times, making certain they were really dead, and then hesitantly put one in my mouth, to the music of my best friend, Jerry, saying, "Yummy, aren't they, Elliot?"

"The best I've had, Jerry. We must come here more often."

The girls? Mine didn't want to see me again. Jerry 's, well he had a fling for a few months. Jerry and I, we're still close friends, but don't ask me why.

A Career Begins
(1964 - age 24)

During senior year we all discussed the job opportunities available. One company paid very well, if you didn't mind relocating to the North Pole. Another company had a great career path, but they were very selective, and scouted the Ivy League schools first. Those were the discussions among the students. Some companies were doing defense work and thus offered draft deferments. My parents thought I was crazy for not pursuing a job that offered a deferment. My attitude was "I love America, and if I'm drafted, I'll serve my country." My mother used to say she loved America too, but she would prefer that someone else serve the country.

Corporations were invited to interview on campus. IBM was there. Even though I had heard that it was the prize corporation to work for, I didn't think it had much to do with me. For one thing, who wanted to live in Poughkeepsie, anyway? My department chairman told me that IBM had a great training program and urged me to sign up for an interview. In actuality I feared I was wasting my time. After all, I still had a slight accent, and furthermore, I hadn't received an "academic" high school diploma. Surely, I thought, mine was an image IBM could do without.

Nevertheless, I interviewed. This led to an invitation to take a test that IBM administered in their Manhattan offices. I was then invited for a second interview in Manhattan, and then finally to visit their facility in Poughkeepsie, NY.

In those few weeks, after successive visits, exposure to their employees, and seeing their way of operating, I became more and more interested in working for them. During this time I had also interviewed with some other companies, including defense contractors. IBM appealed to me the most.

I arrived in Poughkeepsie the night before my final interview and went straight to the hotel that IBM had arranged for me, Howard Johnson's. This, I thought, must be as luxurious as it ever gets. The floor had wall-to-wall carpeting. The hot and cold water were mixed right in the faucet, not in an external adapter that squirted in your face. The air conditioners were built right into the walls and didn't make a sound. The bathroom was devoid of steam pipes passing through to scold me if I got too close. The bathtub was not on legs, but reached right to the floor, with nowhere for the soap to slip under and get lost. And to top it off, this place gave free soap and towels! I had clearly over packed for this trip.

What sheer luxury for someone who lived in a Brooklyn tenement. One could live just in this bathroom, I thought, and be perfectly happy. IBM had advised me that they would reimburse me for all costs relating to this trip. I was told to keep receipts of fares, meals, etc. At dinnertime I went down to the dining room and studied the menu carefully. I was hungry after a long journey, and my eyes went straight to the hearty meat platter. "Yes," I said to the waitress, "I'll have that with the salad, and a large Coke." Immediately I had a change of heart. My God, I thought, when IBM looks at this tab, they'll think I'm one ungrateful pig taking advantage of their generosity! "No, no, come back, please! Make it a cheeseburger and a small Coke."

There were still six months left before graduation, and the job offers were coming in. IBM's offer was considered the prize, so I accepted it. I couldn't wait for the semester to end so that I could go to Poughkeepsie and begin training and working at IBM. I felt like I was getting old. I had lost so much time. After all, I'd be twenty-five years old by graduation.

The graduation ceremony was two weeks after final exams. Why wait? Who wants to wear that silly cap and gown, anyway? The sooner I start working, the sooner I start earning. Packed and ready to go, I finished my last final exam, put down my pen, and left directly for Poughkeepsie.

Career: Poughkeepsie
(1965 - age 25)

Off to IBM, the land of gray suits and soft-spoken voices. By this time I had heard a lot about the IBM image consciousness. In fact, I had already thrown out my sweatshirt, dungarees and sneakers in anticipation.

I was wrong. Things weren't like that for us, the research and development people. IBM had a special tolerance for us and allowed us considerably more latitude. In fact, we had some real gypsies in our department. There was one fellow with a brilliant long red beard and long hair tied in a ponytail. There were also some others in our group who were not quite as radical in style but nevertheless didn't exactly fit the IBM image.

IBM had this dilemma under control. Our building had a main entrance with a lobby and waiting area, but it also had a rear entrance, one much closer to our parking area, that could be opened with our electronic badges. We were never approached about our lifestyles, ponytails, cowboy hats, etc.; on the other hand, no displeasure was shown regarding our slipping in and out of the more conveniently located back door, the one far away from where the IBM sales types, clients and other visitors entered. From the standpoint of image, IBM needed a guy with a ponytail and a cowboy hat walking through the main lobby about as much as a fish needs a bicycle.

The first housing I landed near Poughkeepsie was a furnished room on the second floor over a funeral parlor. This was very convenient, centrally located, yet very quiet. I was going to study a lot, so quiet was desirable.

The entrance to my room was through an exposed staircase in the rear of the house. The funeral parlor activities were conducted at the front of the house, quite separate from my room. I was told that in inclement weather the outside staircase leading directly to my room might freeze over, in which case it was all right to let myself in and out through the inside door leading through the funeral parlor.

On one occasion I found exiting through the rear door to be perilous and headed for the inside staircase. I went down the stairs and opened the door to the parlor. I had expected to see caskets on display. I hadn't expected to see corpses strewn all over the floor in front of me. Apparently, throughout the night dead bodies were dropped off for preparation or embalming the next morning.

The parlor was big, like a banquet room or a dance hall, except that the guests weren't dancing. Or was this in fact life's last dance? If this was the final dance, then it hadn't been handled right. The guests should have been laid out with greater dignity, with their limbs in an orderly array.

People entrust their loved ones with a funeral director, who uses designer words like "dearly departed" and "bereaved." Someone with a demure voice, dark clothes, and special "religious" tones and words makes the shocked relatives understand that everything requires special handling. People pay these parlors to assure a dignified departure for their loved ones. They are not told that the parlor entrusted with the task just dumps them on the floor like a heap of dead dogs.

The scene was very upsetting. Old people who are promised virility are conned, lonely ladies who are promised they'll become dancers are conned. And here at their final ball, impotent and danceless, strewn like rubbish, they're conned out of a dignified departure as well. I was horrified.

The room was cold. A chill went up my spine. In the dim light I negotiated a path from the stairs to the front door, carefully stepping between the bodies. A sleeve got hooked on my shoe. This spooked me a little. This was a party I hadn't been invited to and didn't want to crash. In panic I yanked my foot away, only to pull the hand and body forward with me. I bent over to disentangle myself from the corpse, feeling almost apologetic for not being able to take him with me, to help him escape. I got out of there as fast as I could.

The outside was icy. I now felt cold and gloomy on the inside as well. I've got to snap out of this, I've got to get cheery. IBM doesn't pay me for coming to work looking like death warmed over. Cheer up, Elliot - think about something else. Hmmm... Okay... let's see now. If only I could have borrowed one of those corpses to keep me company under my sister's bed that night. — Stop this nonsense, Elliot! You've got to get to work.

Shortly after this experience I moved to another apartment.

The new apartment had four bedrooms so I grouped up with three others from IBM. Our lifestyles were very similar. Every Friday we all drove to our respective hometowns. Every Sunday night we all returned, each of us first stopping at a supermarket to buy a supply of TV dinners and soda or beer for the week. We all had such similar shopping lists that our freezer looked like a library bookcase. This went on for months until one of our roommates was transferred.

New Roommate
(1965 - age 25)

We posted a sign on the IBM bulletin board and in no time had an applicant for the vacancy. This big, tall, somewhat overweight young man with a very heavy German accent came in. He didn't look one iota like an IBMer. Where did this fellow come from? It turned out he was a pilot who flew IBM's executives to and from Europe on our private jets.

He was a nice enough chap. The roommates and I were to vote him in or out. My roommates, knowing my background, were particularly sensitive to how I would feel about it and gave me a controlling vote. I thought about my feelings, and decided that the Holocaust was not his doing and I was going to grow beyond that sort of bigotry. I voted him in.

We informed him that he was welcome. We also told him that I was Jewish, and he similarly accepted me. He told us that he would move in piecemeal. His plan was to bring back some of his belongings every time he flew to Germany.

A few days later we heard the keys jiggling in the door. Enter Franzel dragging a huge duffel bag behind him. We all greeted him as he started to unpack his bag. He had a store full of big utensils, huge pots and pans. He exclaimed loudly, "I need a pegboard on these walls," and pointed.

It felt almost as if he had commanded that we put up a pegboard on the walls. We decided to humor him and played along. "Yes, Franzel, we'll do it." Except for Franzel, we were all engineers, and putting up a pegboard was well within our capabilities.

Okay, Franzel, a pegboard you shall have. Franzel then announced that he was going out to do some food shopping. The rest of us went about the business of purchasing and mounting a pegboard.

Later that evening he had us peeling, chopping, cutting, slicing and dicing. He made a huge pot of the most magnificent stew that lasted for days. The stock market price per share of TV dinners must surely have plunged that week. Within the next two months each of us put on a good fifteen pounds. In some poetic sense, I thought, this German had saved me from malnutrition.

Franzel did not form close ties with any of us. Oddly enough, the best connection he made seemed to be with me. I knew something about his culture and could also kid him in his own language at times. He knew I was Jewish and he knew I was familiar with Germany, but he didn't know why. He didn't know I had spent my youth in a DP camp. I never discussed that with him. Actually, I avoided discussing anything of that nature with him. I thought it was sufficient that we were both open-minded enough to be roommates. Why push it?

One time one of my more intellectual roommates asked him about how the German youth of today dealt with their history. Franzel blew up. He took the question as a personal assault and went totally out of control, screaming that he was only a child then, that his generation wasn't responsible, and that he was sick and tired of having to answer for the previous generation. He couldn't be stopped. He ranted on about how unfair America was to the Germans, how Americans conspired to make war movies portraying the Germans as total buffoons. When asked why he suspected such a conspiracy, he replied that it was because the Jews with their money and influence controlled the movie industry, as well as our government.

His response drew a total silence from all in the room, particularly the one who asked the question. This volatile subject was never broached again. After that discussion, things reverted to a polite cooperative mode for the next few weeks, until the training program ended and we all went our separate ways.

Things went very well for me at IBM. I completed the training program and was promoted to the Advanced Systems Development Division. I was molding nicely into the IBM way of life. I enjoyed the work, the people, and the country club. Life was very different from the marketplace I knew in Brooklyn. On weekends I went home for love and chicken soup. During the weekdays, I was a WASP in training.

Cousin Babalu
(1965 - age 25)

In a telephone discussion with my mother she said, "By the way, I heard that your cousin Babalu also works for IBM in Poughkeepsie, so if you see him give him regards."

"What, Mom?"

"Yes," she said, "look for Babalu."

"Mom, who is Babalu?"

"Your cousin, Elliot."

"I have a cousin with the name of Babalu?"

"Yes."

"Is he some Latin cousin of ours?"

"No," she explained, "he's American, and his father told me that he works at IBM, too."

"Mom, are these cousins Jewish?"

"What else?" she replied.

"Mom," I said, "Jewish people don't have names like Babalu."

"Yes," she replied, "you have a cousin Babalu."

I gave up and decided my mother was losing it. The strain of my leaving home must have been too much for her. The thought of it! I could just picture Ricky Ricardo announcing, "And here on the bongo drums we have Elliot's cousin Babalu!"

A few months later I was walking down a long corridor at IBM when the person coming toward me yelled out my name. I saw this person approaching me joyously, calling, "Elliot! Don't you recognize me? I'm your cousin Bobby." I vaguely recognized him as a distant cousin I had seen at some family wedding years before. Bobby? That must be Babalu, I thought. Yes, of course, now it all clicked. In Yiddish there is an endearing format for names. If a child's name is Moisha, his mother would call him Moishalu. Okay, so we're in America now, but that's a small detail. If we can mix and match nouns and verbs, it follows that we can add endearing Yiddish endings to American names as well. So if Moisha becomes Moishalu, why can't Bobby become Babalu?

Having finally solved the Babalu mystery, I tried desperately to control myself from bursting out in laughter. All along I had envisioned some mysterious cousin from some unknown Latin branch of the family beating the Bongo drums, screaming "Hay Caramba" and here I was shaking hands with someone who resembled Jackie Mason more than Desi Arnaz.

What's WATT
(1966 - age 26)

I called home from work quite often to chat with my parents. My father nervously kept urging me to keep the conversations short. He was afraid my boss would see me on the phone and fire me. I kept telling him that things weren't like that, that I had a WATTS line and could talk to New York for no charge. He kept insisting the boss would see me and fire me.

One day on the telephone, my father asked me if it was true that IBM was a very important place. I responded that it was a good place to be. "No," he said, "Not just a good place to be, a very important place." It seems someone in his synagogue had inquired about how I was doing, and when my father told him I had graduated from engineering school and was hired by IBM, the man was quite impressed.

Furthermore, my father told me, when the rest of the men in the synagogue heard that I was at IBM, they were also very impressed. How come I didn't tell my own father what an important job I had? Why should he have to find out in the synagogue? Then he asked me what I did for IBM. I told him I would go into it some other time.

During another telephone conversation, my father reminded me that his television was malfunctioning and asked if I could repair it the next time I visited. I urged him to take the TV to a repair shop. He protested vigorously that his own son wouldn't fix his TV set.

"Dad," I pleaded, "I'm not a repairman. I don't have any testing equipment. I'll spend a lot of time and I probably won't know what's wrong with it anyway."

"So what kind of engineer are you, anyway, that you can't fix your father's television? IBM pays you all this money, and you can't fix a simple TV set. So what do you do at IBM, anyway?"

"Dad," I responded, "I don't fix TVs."

"So what do you do at IBM? You can't tell your own father? Everyone in the synagogue knows what their children do, but when they ask me what you do, I don't know what to say."

Giving him a satisfactory answer was complicated. For one thing I had "Confidential Clearance" and really wasn't supposed to discuss my work, as we were constantly briefed. But telling my father, I knew, posed no serious breach of security, as he would most certainly not relate to any of it, nor reiterate it in a meaningful manner.

The difficulty was that my work was very abstract and my father needed a physical example. Dealing with the logic requirements for designing computer language models would make no sense to my father. The fact that I never had to touch a screwdriver was in itself puzzling to him.

"You don't fix computers, you can't fix my TV. What do you do that you can't tell your own father?"

"Dad," I said, "it's just that I don't think I know the Yiddish words to describe it."

"Why won't you tell me?" he kept pestering me. "Is it such secret work? Are you working on our Sputnik?" he asked.

"No, Dad. IBM doesn't build Sputniks."

"You have nothing to do with it?" he asked.

"Well, we do build computers capable of keeping satellites in orbit, Dad."

"You told me you're developing new computers. Will these computers guide our sputniks?" he asked.

"I don't know, Dad. Perhaps."

"Hmmm... now I understand why you can't talk about it."

The next time he spoke to me he posed the following question.

"If one of our Sputniks should fall down, will they know which computer is responsible?"

"What do you mean, Dad?"

"I mean just in case one should fall down, will they know if it's the computer you designed, or one that someone else designed?"

The question of course had no basis in reality, but the implication hurt me deeply. I answered indignantly that if one should fall down it certainly wouldn't be mine. Furthermore, how could he even think that it would be mine?

"It would never be mine, Dad," I said. "How could you even think that it might be mine? I'm the best! I was a good student, and I'm very good here," I responded angrily. The other side of the receiver became silent.

"Dad, don't you know I'm the best? Do you have any doubt about that?" The phone was still quiet. "What is it, Dad? Don't you know I'm the best? Answer me, Dad!"

He finally responded, "Well... you know."

"I know what, Dad?"

"Well," he said, "let's not talk about that." The conversation ended.

The next time I was in Brooklyn, I pursued this topic with my parents once more. I wanted to know what he meant by "Well, you know." My mother and father looked at each other, and my mother finally responded, "Well, you know... the graduation."

"The graduation what?" I asked. "I didn't go to the graduation."

"That's right, you didn't go," they responded.

"So what's your point? You don't think I graduated college?"

"No," they said, "we know you graduated or IBM wouldn't have hired you."

"So what's your point?" I insisted, my frustration mounting.

"So, why didn't you invite us to your graduation?"

"Obviously, because I didn't go."

"But why didn't you go?" they asked.

"I thought you knew that. I didn't go because I was anxious to start working."

"Is that the only reason?" they asked sarcastically.

"What other reason could there be?" I asked.

"Okay," they said, "we don't have to talk about it."

"No, no, I insist, please talk about it. Why do you think I didn't go to graduation?"

"Well, it's obvious. You didn't go so that you wouldn't have to invite us."

"But why wouldn't I want to invite you?" I pleaded.

"So we wouldn't see where you were seated."

"Mom," I cried out, "why would it matter where I was seated?"

"Because it would cause us great shame to see you in the rear row."

At first I had no idea what they were talking about, but then I caught on. It seems that the custom in Poland was that at the graduation ceremony graduates would be assigned seats according to their rank. A seat in the rear would be embarrassing. In some cases students would find an excuse not to attend, thereby saving their family the disgrace. If only I had known that, I would have tried to reserve the first five rows.

My parents never really understood that I had become a good student. They knew I went to college, but they had such a long experience with me as their problem dropout, they assumed that whatever college curriculum I had enrolled in must not have been too demanding. When you take my parents' background and factor in my reputation, their suspicions regarding my academic achievements were not so peculiar.

Trash It
(1966 - age 26)

IBM was very good to me. Within a short time I was moved into the Advanced Systems Development Division at Mohansic Laboratory. But as much as I loved working at IBM, after a year of it I could no longer stand living in the boondocks and wanted to return to New York. My desire to relocate was also boosted by the fact that I had started to seriously date a New York girl. IBM was not conducting any work in Manhattan that was of any interest to me, so I reluctantly left and joined another company.

A necessary byproduct of my upbringing was that I had learned to adapt. When I moved from Poughkeepsie to New York City, I found an affordable apartment in an acceptable neighborhood. The only drawback was that it needed a lot of work. I was up to the task and undertook the renovation.

The work proceeded smoothly, but when I tried to dispose of the construction debris, I was quickly reprimanded and educated in the salient distinction between garbage and trash. The real distinguishing factor, as I understood it, was cost. I was permitted to throw out garbage, but I would have to pay to haul away trash. This seemed both cumbersome and unfair.

Solving this problem required a different approach. I obtained some small cartons from the supermarket and purchased some giftwrap paper. I packed a small carton with trash, giftwrapped it, and placed it outside on the street. In placing it, I favored entrance steps to a brownstone, or next to a bicycle, or someplace where it seemed logical to leave something momentarily.

I then went back to my ground-level apartment and looked out the window. At first nothing happened. Some people would look at the carton, hesitate, and keep on walking. After a few moments a person came by, looked at it, looked about, looked at it again, grabbed it, and ran off with the prize. I repeated this process of giftwrapping my trash and placing it strategically around the neighborhood.

Sometimes it was quick, sometimes it took longer, but in a matter of time, all my trash was stolen.

America, I decided, is an interesting country. It is perhaps the only country in the world where it is easier to acquire things than to dispose of them.

Love Thy Neighbor
(1966 - age 26)

The trash disposed of, the apartment all fixed up, curtains on the windows... Home Sweet Home. This is luxury, America. I now have everything anyone could hope for. My own apartment. Okay, so it was a walk-down, but only four steps. I had two bedrooms and a bathroom. America, what luxury! What waste! My whole family including aunts and uncles could fit in here and there would still be room left over. I wouldn't mind having my aunts here. It's too quiet living all alone. I hate living alone. It's not so bad living with relatives. We did it in Russia and in Germany. I didn't mind it at all.

I decided to put an ad in the Times and find a roommate. I advertised for a friendly male companion to share the apartment. Soon afterward, the doorbell rang. When I opened it, I saw a man standing there with his shirt open and pulled down over one shoulder. "What can I do for you?" I asked.

"Well, isn't that an interesting question!" he responded.

It didn't take me long to see that he had misread my ad. And it seemed many others misread my ad as well. I became aware that the wording used in an ad had to be selected very carefully. Some words in particular seemed to be trigger words. My mistake was that I said I wanted a "friendly" roommate. I didn't mean that friendly. I promptly changed the ad and found a serious-minded roommate who wanted a room and nothing more.

Marriage

(1967 - age 27)

I was almost twenty-seven years old. I had a good job and an apartment in the city. What else did I need? Yes, a nice Jewish girl to marry.

A year earlier, during the fall of 1965, I went to a Chanuka party at New York University. On the same evening there was another dance going on across the hall. The other dance was held by a Latin group. Throughout the evening I shuttled from one dance to the other. I didn't feel like I belonged at either dance, but the Latin music was so much better. The Latins were much livelier, too. I spent most of the evening at the Latin dance. In the last moments of the evening, I went back to where I was supposed to be, the Chanuka dance.

As the last dance began to play, I noticed Ellen, sitting in a corner, alone. I was drawn by her thick straight dark hair, visualizing it pulled tightly into a bun, like a flamenco dancer. I would have thought that she had strayed in from the Latin party, except for her beautiful blue eyes. We danced.

Ellen was only seventeen and a half, shy and innocent. We shared history and our infatuation with Mexico. She had spent the previous summer with relatives in Mexico City.

This was an obvious match. I knew hers was the right family for me because they drank tea out of a glass, instead of a cup (something one learns in Europe). It was love all around. I loved Ellen, Ellen loved me, her father was a doctor, the windows had curtains, her parents were European, my parents loved her parents, everybody loved everybody. Everyone was happy to see me marry a Jewish girl. Just one little ceremony, and I can bring happiness to so many people... my parents, relatives, friends, neighbors, synagogue members, not to mention the whole Jewish race.

This was it. This was the America I was promised. This made the picture complete. I was held in high esteem for my ability to entertain my in-laws in a few languages. Even though I wasn't a doctor, an engineer was adequate. Besides, her father was a doctor, so he knew the profession wasn't all it was cracked up to be.

At nineteen the bride was so young. Except for her visit to Mexico, she had only lived with her parents and had negligible life experiences of her own. I loved her, and yet I was undoubtedly marrying the image her family projected as much as her. After all, it was the family home I visited. It was neat, it always smelled of good food, it had warm inviting curtains on the windows. But who was responsible the way the home felt, was it she or her parents? Did it matter?

If it did matter, I wasn't going to find out. Though I was older than the bride chronologically and certainly more accomplished, emotionally I was still rather young. My intense focus on educating myself for a career had robbed me of some emotional development. What did I look at? Did I consider the kind of life I envisioned for myself? Would I be content with a housewife? Did I need a career woman as a mate? Did I need a person in whom I could entrust my life, or did I need someone that would just adore and worship me? I never answered any of these questions. I never even understood enough to ask them. The silky hair, the blue eyes, those were the things that I noticed. Wasn't it that way for everyone?

Moving
(1967 - age 27)

We became engaged. Ellen's mother took the job of arranging a wedding very seriously. She was, after all, a doctor's wife. One mustn't ignore one's station in life. Who's the best caterer, where are the nicest flowers? Doing things that are "correct" is a full time job.

Speaking about correct, her mother was quick to point out that it wasn't fitting for a doctor's daughter to live in a dingy walk-down apartment on East 27th Street. She was accustomed to better. After being needled about this a few times, I decided to search for another apartment. But what could I afford? I had only been working for two years. I didn't have a doctor's income, and Manhattan was so expensive.

"Co op for sale. Owners have to dispose of studio on Sutton Place. $7,000, low maint." The price was right, but this Sutton Place, I thought, must be a real dumpy street. When I got there, I realized Sutton Place wasn't dumpy at all. The apartment was a bright studio with a river view. It was, however, in shambles. The owners were anxious and offered generous financing terms. Still, even the two-thousand-dollar down payment had to be borrowed from the bank.

When we told Ellen's parents that I bought a co op on Sutton Place, they were thrilled. This was exactly where their daughter had been raised to live. My father saw things differently.

"Hello, Dad, guess what, your son bought a place to live."

"How much did it cost you?"

"Seven thousand dollars!"

"A how-many-family did you buy?"

"Dad, it's just one apartment!"

"So much for just one apartment, son? That's a lot of money! So how big is this apartment, how many rooms?"

"Dad, it's just one room, but it's beautiful."

"Just one room? Are you crazy, son? Here in Brooklyn I can get you a forty-two-family house with a seven-thousand-dollar down payment."

Evenings and weekends I worked on the apartment. I built a wall to create a separate bedroom area. I spackled, painted, rewired the outlets. Ellen kept me company and kept me company and kept me company. Well, after all, I was the more skilled one. I knew how to do these things.

"While I'm painting, why don't you clean the kitchen cabinets, they're filthy. Here's some Ajax, Brillo, sponges."

"You want me to do that?"

"Of course!"

Meanwhile her parents called to chat. When her parents learned about my enslaving their daughter, they came over right away. I thought I would never hear the end of it.

"My dear young man, our daughter's hands were made for playing the piano, not for scrubbing with Brillo!"

"Then who is supposed to do that?" I asked. "I work all day, I go to graduate school in the evening and every spare moment left, I do the construction here. Ellen just goes to school, and spends her free time here just keeping me company. If she can't clean the kitchen, who should?"

"A maid, my dear young man! That's what maids are for. Everyone on Sutton Place has a maid! Nobody lives here and doesn't have a maid! I'm surprised you don't know that, Elliot."

Ellen was young and totally dominated by her parents. I was in love and not completely sure of what was right. The opinion of the three of them, one of whom was a doctor, yet - well, it overwhelmed me. Shame on me. How could I ask my young bride to scrub cabinets? There must be something wrong with me. You can take a boy out of DP camp, but you can never take the DP mentality out of the boy. This is not DP camp, this is America, this is Sutton Place. I had better shape up.

Naturally, I couldn't afford a maid, so I worked into the night and scrubbed the kitchen cabinets myself, then went back to painting the wall. Unfortunately, I didn't see the writing on it.

The wedding was held at the Hotel Delmonico. It was a cut above the type of reception I used to crash as a teenager in Brooklyn. Every so often I amused myself by letting my eyes scour the room, especially eyeing the kiddies' table, to see if there were any strange faces or party crashers. I felt I should be able to spot one, if there were any, for, after all, who in the world had more experience in this field than I? I envisioned spotting one, and asking him to sit at the dais with me as a distinguished guest of honor.

Vice President
(1968 - age 28)

I adjusted to New York, to my new job, and to my marriage very well. It was three years after my graduation. I was a department manager at a small computer firm and life couldn't have been better. Actually, that isn't completely true. Life could have been better.

The president of the company, who was also a major shareholder, one day decided I was the perfect man to manage the sales department. I thought he had lost his marbles. But he kept insisting that I was doing a great job and therefore was the right man to step into this position. Never mind that I had had nothing to do with marketing or sales. I was running technical departments. Strictly technical. No, he insisted. He said he could see that I had the fiber to do equally well at any position. So it went... He kept offering the job, and I kept rejecting it.

He pleaded that we weren't breaking the "nut" and that we needed somebody new to manage sales. He asked me to help him interview people for this position. I didn't know what the "nut" meant, and I didn't care, but I did agree to help him interview someone to take over sales. As we interviewed, we discussed the prospects. He kept pointing out that none of them were acceptable and kept insisting that I take it.

Finally, one day he became very persistent. He wouldn't let me out of the office, insisting that I had to take the job.

"Why?" I pleaded.

"Because we're not breaking the nut."

"What in hell is the nut?" I asked, "and what does that have to do with me?"

"The 'nut' means expenses," he responded. "We are not covering expenses. The fact that you're doing a great job is meaningless, because we are going to fold if our income does not exceed expenses."

I had no idea we were on the brink of folding. Why didn't he tell me that when he hired me three months previously? Well, now that I understood the "nut" problem, I was more open to talk about the job.

"So," I said, "what's the deal? What are you offering me?" He offered an immediate raise of a couple of thousand dollars per year and an improved title. The following week, I was to go to Washington to attend a special sales training seminar that presumably would give me all the knowledge necessary to get started with my new responsibility.

I told him his deal was unacceptable. "Why should I leave what I liked doing to enter an area I knew nothing about for a couple of thousand dollars raise?"

"What do you want?" he asked.

So I told him what I wanted. "First of all, to become the VP of the company."

"That's pushing it a little, don't you think?" he said. But he agreed to it.

"Secondly, I want the raise you offered but also a percentage of sales in excess of the nut."

"You son-of-a-bitch!" he exploded. "That's why you were holding out all this time. You want to take me to the cleaners!"

Tempers cooled, we made the deal and had a big lunch to celebrate. I took my training in Washington, returned, and went about rebuilding company sales.

Within two months things were terrific. The company was making money, my compensation had doubled, and the president was beside himself. With me running the shop he began to show up less and less. He'd stay out playing and drinking and show up only every couple of days, insisting that we have a lavish lunch and telling me how miraculous all this was.

In two more months, my compensation had again climbed substantially. Now I thought he'd be the most grateful man in the world. It didn't work out that way. He'd come in, not completely sober, and still take me out for lunch, but spit his venom. He decided that I was making much too much money. Why should a kid only twenty-seven years old be making such outrageous amounts of money?

I asked him if I wasn't doing a good job, if he wasn't happy with me. No, none of the above. I just shouldn't be making that much money. He felt he must have been crazy to enter into such a deal with me. I objected. But he had the final say, and he fired me.

I went home that evening totally devastated. Such a quick rise, and an equally quick downfall! I sat in quiet despair for a while, then decided to write an updated resume. The next morning, as I was getting dressed to go out job hunting, I got a phone call. It was from my former secretary. She informed me that the president expected me in at 10:00 a.m. for a meeting. I told her she must be mistaken; there would be no more meetings. I had been fired. No, the president was standing beside her and asked that I please come in. I came in. He apologized to me for being foolish, ungrateful, and unwise and rehired me.

This same scenario repeated itself two more times in the succeeding months. After the third time I decided that I had to find other employment.

Insecure

The repeated hirings, firings and rehirings reawakened many insecurities within me, resulting in painful, realistic dreams, almost hallucinations. In my dreams, I would get a letter from Pratt Institute that read something like this:

Dear Mr. Rais:

In a routine inspection of old records we regraded one of your exams in thermodynamics. We noticed that we scored it improperly, and that you should not have passed. As a result, you should not have graduated. Please mail back your degree.

Yours truly,

By this time in my life, I was already accomplished and respected by my peers. I had also been the vice president of a company. Yet the sense prevailed that I was a big fraud because I had never earned an academic high school diploma, and therefore I was undeserving of all this. I always felt that I would somehow be discovered, stripped, and returned to Russia to eat bugs again.

I had risen too fast and hadn't been at it long enough to justify such remuneration. Nor had I been at it long enough to present a good record of achievement. I had become somewhat of a square peg, and it was difficult for me to adjust to the round holes of the work force. I worked for another, much larger, corporation for a little while, but began to feel very empty because I wasn't doing anything creative. No research, no computers. I had outgrown this, and was basically running businesses. I used to think that what I finally wound up doing was not too different from my father's store. I was, after all, running a business. I was buying, selling, and making money. Why on earth did I knock my brains out with all this education? Attaining my education required such a heroic effort, and now it looked as if I had thrown it all away.

On one level, my personal life was enviable. With my wife and two children, I moved to a beautiful house on an acre of land in a plush suburb outside of New York City. And yet something was troubling me at the time, as illustrated by this little story.

At the age of three my son spent much of his time playing in our yard. One time I caught him stalking a little ant with a knife. As the ant climbed onto the driveway, he cut it in half. When I asked him why, he responded that he was fascinated by the way each half sometimes walked off in different directions. As I watched him, I recalled my own childhood in Russia. We now lived in a beautiful house on an acre of land in a plush New York suburb, far away from Agdam. My children also stalked bugs, but not out of hunger. I didn't want that to ever happen, not during my life, not afterwards.

The fear that my wife could not continue to propagate and preserve what I had so painstakingly built ultimately became a destructive element in our marriage. I didn't feel my wife could maintain what I had created. The burden was all on my shoulders. I felt like I didn't have a partner to share this with. I needed changes in my life. I decided to leave industry altogether and go into teaching at a university.

Teaching
(1971 - age 31)

It was 1971, only ten years after I had entered Pratt Institute. Things had changed - the Vietnam war and the drug culture were now raging. Vacant spots and liberalized and open admissions policies were in effect at technical colleges. Whereas I had struggled to get into and stay in engineering school, some of these kids were there simply because it was available; some were there to please their parents, others to stay out of Vietnam. I dealt with students who could take it or leave it, or at least so it seemed.

I taught courses in calculus and computer science at Newark College of Engineering. My challenge was to stimulate the students, but how? Calculus doesn't just pop into one's head. These are not intuitive subjects; they require hard work and real motivation. These students had no interest in the classical textbook problems. I observed the students' lives more closely and began to fashion problems that had greater relevance to them.

I noticed they played a lot of pool between classes. Terrific, I thought. I could create problems on the pool table. Show them how with the knowledge of calculus, some physics formulae, and the computer, their performance on the pool table could improve, as well as their understanding of the subject. This proved a terrific success. Kids who initially sat in the last rows of the classroom were suddenly hustling to sit up front so as not to miss a word.

With this approach, the classes became more fun for the students, and thus more rewarding for me. As the semester wound down I still had the responsibility, according to the syllabus, of teaching them one business application of the computer. I did this by asking each student to model a plan to embezzle a company using the computer. This problem created the greatest interest of all, but it was to cause me some grief a few years later.

One benefit of teaching is long vacations. In 1972, during my stint at Newark College, my wife and I spent the whole summer in Europe. I had a real need to see Europe again as an adult. Feeling that I wasn't yet ready to enter Germany, I first went to England, Switzerland, Italy, then back to Switzerland.

Given my fondness for aesthetics and order, I naturally favored Switzerland. After staying in a hotel in Zurich for a week, we realized that the most scenic part of Zurich was by the lake. We saw a camping site adjacent to the lake and decided it would be more fun to go camping than stay in our sterile hotel room.

Neither I nor my wife had ever camped before, so we stopped by a department store and, with the help of an eager saleslady, bought a tent and everything else we would need. When we returned to our hotel, I decided to assemble the tent right in our room, to see if we could manage it under controlled conditions, with good lighting and ample time to read the foreign-language instructions.

We were on the ground level of an Old-World type hotel. Our room had French doors leading to a courtyard garden. We closed the doors and drew the curtains, so as not to upset the management. Safe from potential embarrassment, we assembled the tent in our room, examined the other equipment, and were content that we could manage in the wilderness.

The next day we checked out of the hotel and into the campground, a few hundred feet from the hotel and directly adjacent to the Zurich lake (not exactly the wilderness).

Late that night, before we bedded down, I checked out the facility very carefully. I became aware that it was a very large campsite, accommodating hundreds of people. I noticed that even though there were many sinks for washing up, there were only two shower stalls for the whole camp. I made a mental note to get up very early the next morning so that I could be one of the fortunate ones to take a shower. I made sure I had the proper coins to deposit for hot water.

I had no alarm clock, and my internal clock failed me. As my eyes opened I could see the sun shining brightly through my tent. I could hear the sounds of many people outside. It seemed that everyone had arisen before me. Disappointed, I dragged myself to the bathroom, resigned to the fact that a shower was clearly going to be out of the question that morning.

As I approached the service area, I was startled to discover that both showers were empty. I stood in amazement, thinking that perhaps I still hadn't woken up. Looking around, I noticed that there were many people waiting in line for the sinks. Further observation revealed a most interesting phenomenon. As people reached the sinks, each person in turn washed a particular part of his or her body. One person washed only his face. One person washed his face and his feet. Another washed his face and his chest. Yet another washed only his underarms.

By this time I had become very American, and I was conditioned to taking a daily shower. It hadn't occurred to me how inefficient that was. The Europeans had it down to a science. After all, if only the underarms are dirty, why wash the whole body?

Yes, I had become very American. I had long forgotten how scarce resources were in the rest of the world. I had forgotten that it is not a birthright to take an hour-long hot shower, as one does in the States whenever one feels like it.

During our trip to Europe, I was faced with a dilemma. Was I or was I not going to visit Germany? I'm just a tourist, I reminded myself. They're not going to punish me or detain me. What am I so worried about? After a month of camping throughout Europe, it seemed time to see Germany, if I were to see it at all before my vacation was over.

We entered Germany through Switzerland's Lake Constance region. I drove a few miles, then pulled in for gas. The attendant was polite enough, but when he gave me the change, he said, "Have a good fart."

I was momentarily startled. He knows, I thought - is my history written all over my face? This impudent son-of-a-bitch is insulting me! I caught my breath and finally realized that "fart" in German means "ride." The chap was simply wishing us a good ride. Calm down, Elliot. I was so defensive that I had a hair trigger.

We drove deeper into Germany, revisited the Munster Kirche, and finally reached the DP camp, or what used to be the DP camp. Now a cluster of townhouses stood on the site. They looked like any middle class condominium development. No communal baths, no shoichets, no MP. It was as if they had never existed. Just people going about their lives. Some German must have gone to the planning board very much as I do here, and gotten approval for these townhouses, the same way I would, and he did in Germany what I do in the States. There was only one difference - I get yelled at if I want to cut down one tree, and he removed a whole history. He bulldozed away my entire past.

I drove on and found a camping site for the night. We arrived at the campsite late and in the middle of a rainstorm. My wife and I had practiced putting up the tent many times, and, in a pinch, could do it in thirty seconds, perfect for a rainstorm. I stopped the car, pulled out the tent gear, and gave my wife her parts for assembly. As I was starting to break the speed record, she just froze and said, "No, Elliot, let's pitch the tent over there where it's nicer."

I screamed over the sound of the rain, "We're getting soaked! This is no time to be picky!"

But she wouldn't hear of it. In no mood to argue, I yielded, picked up the pieces that I had already dropped, and, totally drenched, sloshed over to her chosen spot. We pitched the tent and climbed into our sleeping bags.

I tossed and turned the whole night, with an inexplicable fear. I could not sleep at all. The following morning we were treated to a splendid sunrise that revealed majestic, distant mountains. We now had a better view of the campsite and the charming chalet adjacent to it. We visited the chalet for breakfast and sat beside a picture window that faced the magnificent landscape.

As the proprietress served us, we remarked on the campsite's beauty. She in turn commended our choice of campsite. She proudly proclaimed that its beauty was well known, and that we had in fact camped on what used to be Hitler's favorite campsite.

As if the sun had passed behind a cloud, the place suddenly lost its beauty. She might have wondered why we failed to convey how honored we were to have our good taste validated by none other than Hitler himself. We promptly left.

After returning to the United States from our vacation, I taught for an additional year. I had earned a masters degree in engineering at NYU and was about to commence a doctoral program in order to advance in the teaching profession, but decided that this life would be too limiting for me. Although it satisfied a need to be involved in a scholarly activity, I felt I wasn't growing.

The study of engineering just wasn't what it used to be. The environment didn't feel sufficiently academic. I felt that the open admissions policy had reduced the quality of the engineering students and the curriculum. When I tried to hold to certain academic standards, I was reminded by the department head that I had to work with what I had. Even though some students entered engineering school through alternate admissions, and had a very poor grasp of algebra, geometry and trigonometry, I had to adjust my calculus curriculum so that these students could keep up, too. I was faithful to the department directive, but felt that I was cheating the better students, the ones who were prepared and capable. They were being robbed of some of the finer nuances of the subject.

I was also becoming aware of the pettiness of the administrative machine. I began to miss the high-rolling corporate life.

My colleagues knew that I had been successful in industry, and I felt they were defensive towards me, as if to justify their being career teachers. As if it was necessary to explain or to prove to me that it was not true that "Those who can't, - teach." I was not easily accepted into the circle.

I altered the curriculum to better motivate the students, and there was a definite improvement, but I could not make up for the years of preparation that some of my students lacked, and this frustrated me. Meanwhile, the commute into and out of Newark concerned me. I didn't feel safe. This was beginning to preoccupy me. I began to dream about a career change. I was tiring of teaching and I had also tired of working for others. It was time to start my own business.

I would have preferred to teach for another few years, until I felt more secure about going out on my own. However, a certain incident accelerated my departure from the university.

My teaching load was three courses per semester. At least one was always a graduate course that I had to teach in the late afternoon or early evening. The drive to the university was mostly on major highways except for the last mile or so, which was through a dark, rundown section of the city. Once inside the campus gates, one felt more secure.

One winter evening, driving home from the university, my car broke down. This was particularly ironic since I had had my car serviced that same day, while I was teaching. What's more, there had been nothing wrong with my car. I had brought it in for servicing simply as insurance. It had been running so well for such a long time, I thought I'd better get a tune-up, just so that I wouldn't get stuck on the road going home some day.

In any case, my car died on a dark street in the middle of nowhere. No, not in the middle of nowhere, for I saw a gas station about a block and a half up the road. I started walking to the gas station to call the mechanic that had serviced the car. I had a few things to tell him, but most of all I wanted to tell him to come and tow me back to the university. The university had special dorms where I could sleep over in a pinch. This was a pinch.

The gas station was not well-lit, but I did spot the phone. I also saw three guys hanging around, doing what, I wasn't sure. They may have been pitching pennies or something. I didn't want to look. I didn't want to provoke them. I hurried into the phone booth to make my call. I was very nervous. I made my call in a hurry, trying not to see what was happening outside.

It was hard to avoid. The voices got louder and louder. Now they were leaning against the phone booth, making jokes, laughing. There were three of them. They were tall, lean, bruised, dirty and rough-looking. One of them was playing with a knife, cleaning his fingernails with it. He proclaimed, "Whah we gonna do to the white f——er in the phone booth?"

I was sure I was dead. Agdam, Munich, Brooklyn, Poughkeepsie. Illiteracy, night school, day school, a life full of ambition, causes and struggles, and it's all over in a phone booth? I came such a long way, just to die in vain in Newark, New Jersey? To die for no particular cause or reason at all?

There was no time to waste. I could call the police, but I'd be a puddle of blood before I finished dialing. A bluff was my only hope. They didn't want my money; this was not a robbery. They wanted amusement. Could I redirect their energies? I had to try something; my life depended on it. Could I hold my knees steady long enough to try this? I was scared.

I slammed down the receiver and slammed open the phone booth door. One guy almost fell into the booth. I yelled at them, "Hey man, I need some strong dudes to push my car into this station." They stood still for a moment. "Are you mother-ers gonna stand here and play with your f—king knives, or are you gonna show me you can push some metal? C'mon guys, follow me." My heart felt like it was going to jump out of my body.

I started toward my car, pointing at it. "Come on," I yelled at them again. "I haven't got all night."

"Yeah man, let's help this dude," one of them responded.

Maybe this was going to work. I got calmer and started to reinforce our association. As we walked along, I asked them what kind of pool they shot. I told them math had improved my students' game.

They pushed the car in to the garage for me and stayed with me until the tow truck came. I was safe now. No one would bother me with my new protectors.

I finally got towed back to the university and received a lift home from a colleague. On the way home, my knees started shaking again. Imagine me calling those guys mother—ers! They could have killed me on the spot! Was I brave or was I an asshole? Maybe if I survived it I was brave, and if they had killed me I would have been a dead asshole? I could just see the headlines the next morning. "Asshole professor provokes three armed thugs by calling them mother—ers, and is naturally and deservedly killed on the spot."

Just the previous summer, I had responded to an incident in a characteristically opposite manner - like a complete coward. During the vacation in Europe on a beautiful summer day in Zurich, and I went down to the lake for a swim. As I was swimming, a ducklike creature approached me and hissed. I playfully hissed back. It hissed again, this time more aggressively, and began to approach me. I retreated gracefully, still hissing back.

When I exited the water, this fowl kept following me, hissing aggressively. This is embarrassing, I thought. Am I running from a duck?

This swanlike creature assumed new dimensions once out of the water. This was Superswan, or Superduck, or something! I didn't know a swan could be that big - bigger than me.

The pace quickened. The swan was taking bigger strides and I was half running, trying not to run too fast, embarrassed to death that I was running from a swan, hoping anxiously that no one I knew would see me. I felt like a stupid coward, nevertheless, I ran.

And to think that I had just called these dangerous thugs mother—ers. The following morning I handed in my resignation at the school. I offered to finish out the semester, but I would not return the following year.

Who could have dreamed that the term "mother—ker," the very first expression I heard when I put my feet on American soil, would save my life one day.

Building

(1873 - age 33)

It was time to decide what to do for a living. Ever since I had played with Erector sets as a child, I had wanted to design and build structures. I had already worked in the fields of engineering and computer science. They were fun, rewarding and lucrative, but I really wanted to build homes.

A distant cousin of my father's had been a very prosperous builder. This cousin used to visit us in the DP camp in Germany during his frequent world excursions. The curious thing was that even though he was a multimillionaire and we were virtually destitute, when he visited us my parents and my aunts made a huge fuss over him. They cooked, they baked, they escorted him to Munich so he and his wife could go shopping. My parents used to pay his train fare to Munich.

I couldn't understand this. He was so rich, and yet my parents paid his fare. When I asked why he was so rich, my parents explained that he was a builder. When I asked why we had to pay his fare, they answered, "Out of respect." I wondered if it was respect for his being a builder or for his wealth.

I still remembered this man. I didn't want to be like him, but the memory of his independence at a time when the rest of us were living on Spam and Carnation milk was still with me.

I decided to become a builder. Before my teaching commitment was over, I had ample time to begin construction activity on the side. I began to prepare for the transition. I hung out at construction sites, talked to contractors, attended building association meetings, studied the market, and shopped for a parcel of land on which I could learn to build.

I got my feet wet by purchasing a rundown two-family home and renovating it with my own hands. Soon after, I purchased a six-unit building that had suffered an explosion from a dry-cleaning tenant. I renovated that building, but contracted about half of the work to skilled labor. By then I had developed sufficient confidence to try building a house from the ground up.

I found an inexpensive piece of land and began building. This first small home took me a full year to build. I built a little, stopped, learned a little, stopped. I had to proceed slowly in order to match my income with construction expenditures. The banks did not wish to finance a builder in training, although as the house neared completion, I was able to get some money from the bank for the final construction costs.

The home building business has been interesting for me. It is like playing with blocks. As business grew, I started designing my homes as well. I had always wanted to be an architect, and now I had someone to commission me - me! I've remained in the construction business to this day.

(1974 - age 34)

Although I thought I knew my parents well, I could still be taken aback from time to time by the culture gap between us. Even after years in this country, they still saw the world differently.

One day my father wanted to see one of my projects, the wreck that I had renovated. I, of course, was most pleased to show it to him. I wanted my father to be proud of my achievement. He had been very skeptical of my wisdom in leaving IBM, and then the university, "to go and dig ditches," as he said.

I took him to the small commercial building that I had restored after the dry-cleaning explosion and showed him around. I showed him the rebuilt stores and offices. He commented upon how nice it all looked. He thought I had utilized the space well.

To show my dad just how clever his son was, I took him to the basement. I even had a tenant there. This fellow imported and sold salt water tropical fish wholesale. He received beautiful rare species a few at a time, airlifted from their exotic waters. Because of the weight of the water tanks, my basement was an ideal place for him.

My father walked around from tank to tank, looking at the fish. He asked me if this tenant managed to pay his rent. I responded that the tenant did indeed pay his rent, and on time. My father said he didn't understand it. How could the tenant make enough money from these little fish to pay such a rent? I told my father that these little fish were very expensive. My father stopped at a tank, pointed to a particularly rare fish, and asked me, "How much, for instance, does this fish cost?"

I happened to know the price and answered, "Five hundred dollars."

"What crazy people would pay five hundred dollars a pound for fish?" my father asked.

When I told him that was the price for a single fish, he shook his head and muttered, "Crazy Americans."

Haunted
(1978 - age 38)

About five years after I quit teaching, I received a phone call. "Mr. Rais, this is Attorney So-and-so. Show up in the courthouse tomorrow, 9:00 a.m." I wanted to know why. He wouldn't tell me.

I couldn't imagine what they wanted from me. The watches? After all those years they found out about the watches? Impossible.

Before returning from that European vacation, during a phone conversation to the States, I was reminded that watches were a bargain in Switzerland. So there I was, arriving back to America with watches. (Some things never change.) We had the two watches that we had come to Europe with, two that we had purchased for ourselves, and four more as presents for our parents. I looked for a secure way to transport these watches back to the States. The simplest way would be to wear all eight of them up my arm, under my jacket. I felt so proud to have discovered this new method of safekeeping. After all, thieves go for your wallet. Who was going to climb up my sleeve?

Once at Kennedy Airport, I had to go to the bathroom. As I was about to enter, a man approached me and whispered, "Hey, man, you wanna buy a chain?" He opened his jacket to reveal a storeful of presumably hot gold chains.

I couldn't resist. I immediately rolled up my sleeve and countered, "No, thanks. How about you? Wanna buy a watch?" The look on this guy's face was priceless.

At the time I thought this was very funny, but after the initial laugh I started to worry. How stupid of me, I thought. How must this appear? What if someone saw me and thought I was selling stolen watches? Worse yet, what if someone thought I was smuggling? Surely that was a crime worse than selling knishes on the beach. These thoughts returned to preoccupy me after I received this mysterious phone call.

No, it couldn't be, nobody saw that, did they? No, that's impossible, nobody knows about that. In any case, I didn't do anything illegal, so what am I worried about?

Nevertheless, I couldn't wait until the next day. I called the attorney and insisted that he tell me why I was wanted in court. He asked me if I had ever had a particular student in my class while I was teaching. Some of my classes were quite popular and held in very large lecture halls, so I couldn't remember all my students' names, but he refreshed my memory. Yes, I vaguely remembered that student.

"Fine," he said. "You are hereby asked to appear in court tomorrow morning."

"I'm busy designing houses. What if I can't appear?

"Then we will have to subpoena you."

I was up all that night, and the only thing I could think of was the embezzlement problem that I had taught my students. Yes, that must be it. I had taught them how to embezzle, and one of my jerky students took it seriously and acted on it. That student really wanted value for his tuition. It had to be one of my dumber students, too, because he had obviously done it wrong if he had gotten caught.

It turned out that the student had done no such thing. This student was even dumber than I thought.

He was accused of stealing television sets from his employer, who manufactured them. The attorney was trying to paint a picture of a nice scholarly-type kid, a teacher's pet, and was hoping that good old Professor Rais would help him do that.

Still, all night I worried that one of my jerky students had pulled off an embezzlement and that I had been named as an accomplice for having taught him how to embezzle. Once again, I felt that old fear, and dreamed those old dreams of being apprehended, stripped of my citizenship, not to mention my degrees, and shipped right back to Russia to eat bugs.

Separation and Divorce
(1980 - age 40)

My marriage wasn't a bad marriage, but the seeds of destruction were built in. It lasted twelve years and two wonderful children before it cracked. No, she wasn't a bad wife, either, and certainly not a bad person. She was simply the only child of parents who wouldn't let go. There were many recurring situations early in our relationship that made me feel like I had to do it all alone. Abandoned, like the child in the Russian forest.

If only I had the wisdom then to move her three thousand miles from her parents, perhaps Ellen and I might still be together. But I didn't have that wisdom. My relationship with my wife and children was very close. I was very much a family person, and I flourished with the love all around me. Yet the differences that had been there at the outset were

259

still there a dozen years later. Nothing had changed. In fact, it seemed as though nothing at all could change about anything.

My career was going great. I felt as if there was nothing at all I couldn't achieve. There was virtually nothing I couldn't have. Yet I felt insecure. I felt that if something happened to me, the family would fall apart. How would they get by?

I couldn't imagine my wife ever taking a job. She had no interest in working. Although we had no need for extra money, I urged her to take a job, even a part-time job, to develop a marketable skill. She refused. She insisted that her job was in the home, that she was perfectly happy there and saw no point in working.

It seemed important to me. I felt that I had worked hard to establish what I had. Somehow I had to be reassured that it would all remain intact, that it would survive even if I didn't. What if something happened to me? My wife knew nothing about working, running a business, or investing money. After such hard work to build it all, how could I stand to watch it crumble? Wait a minute. We're talking about if I die? If I die, I won't see anything crumbling. Well, that's only a detail. It doesn't matter if I see it or not, I'll somehow know anyway. And it's haunting me while I'm alive. Wait a minute, I need to control that situation, too. I've controlled everything in my life. I must be able to control events even after I pass on. What would happen to my two precious children? The pressure was too great. I left.

Relationships are complex. I can't say that I was right and she was wrong, nor the other way around. Besides, I don't think it's ever about who's right and who's wrong. Actually, some of the very things I despised about her, I also envied. She was complacent. She was happy being home, taking care of the children. I'm restless and ambitious. What's so great about that? She was content, never seeming to worry, always knowing that everything would somehow turn out okay, that someone would always take care of her, of us. She believed that if I didn't take care of us, then somehow the universe would.

I was driven, concerned. I felt that if I didn't take care of things, I'd be back in the street. She never worried about the future. I did.

I said in the beginning that we shared history. Not as much as I wanted to believe. We were brought into and brought up in this world in such completely different ways that we could never relate to it in the same way.

In leaving the marriage I also left behind all sense of purpose. I lost all interest in work. What was there to work for? Who was I working for? I had sufficient means to just float. What was the purpose of striving for more?

I found it unbearable to remain in the same suburban community. There were too many reminders. I was a productive member of the community. I had built many homes, and many people knew me. Certainly the trade community knew me. I was a heavy consumer of everything: lumber, hardware, concrete, legal services, real estate services. I appeared in front of the zoning boards and planning boards of many of our neighboring communities. The local newspaper would document my appearances and my projects. It felt like everybody knew me. I could barely go out of my house without being greeted by someone, or running into someone while waiting for a light to change. "Hello, Elliot, how's the Missus? How are those adorable children of yours?" I would nod my head, roll the car window up, and drench my steering wheel with tears. I loved what I had created and I was losing it all. I was destroying it.

I was now forty years old, a time of midlife crisis for many. There were real things in my marriage that were troublesome, yet I'm sure that my midlife passage, though I can't credit it with all of my turmoil, was certainly contributing to my volatility.

The possibility that this temporary emotional upheaval might irrevocably alter the rest of my life was particularly troublesome for me. What if there really was nothing wrong with my marriage? What if it was just midlife crisis?"

After we separated, I thought about this night and day, every waking moment. This was by far the worst period of my life. I was accustomed to being decisive. I could make decisions about anything in seconds. That was no problem for me. I needed no consensus, no second opinion. I knew what I was doing. I couldn't do wrong. Now, for the first time in my life, I couldn't decide on anything.

I wanted out, but I didn't want out. I wanted divorce and I didn't want it. I teetered on the fence for a year and a half after our separation. I couldn't go either way, and I was in total agony.

One day, in my therapist's office, I burst into uncontrollable tears, crying like a child.

"What is it, Elliot?"

"I am so wimpy."

"Why?"

"Because I'm stuck."

"What do you mean?"

"Well, it's been one and a half years now since we separated and I still can't go forward, nor can I go back to her. This is a miserable place I'm at."

"Elliot," he said, "why do you want to be there?"

"What do you mean," I asked. "I don't want to be there."

"Then why don't you move forward?" he asked.

"I can't."

"So why don't you go back?" he asked,

"I can't."

"So you want to remain on the fence, Elliot. Why do you want to be on the fence?"

"I don't! No! I hate being on the fence more than anything!"

"Then go someplace, it doesn't matter where. If being on the fence is worse than anything, then anywhere you go will be better. And if it's the wrong way for you, you'll just have to change again."

Suddenly it all connected. That made total sense. I proceeded with the divorce.

Single in NY: Floating
(1982 - age 42)

Nothing in my life prepared me for the experience of divorce. No pain equaled it. After my separation, I moved back to New York City to figure out what it was all about. In so doing, I stopped the serious business of building homes and floated for a while, engaging in various little endeavors that served to preoccupy me during this turmoil.

First, I got an apartment. When I ordered my telephone, New York Telephone talked me into ordering their new miracles, call waiting and call forwarding as well. Within a week, I discovered that every single New Yorker had a telephone answering machine. I was convinced it was the law, kind of like the law about carrying a draft card for those over eighteen. I can just hear the conversation.

"Officer, honest, I was making a right turn here because I live on this block."

"Yeah, you don't look to me like someone who lives in New York."

"Here, officer, look, here's my Citicard, and my receipt for a telephone answering machine."

"Good enough for me."

So many new things to keep me busy, like programming my answering machine. The instruction manual had been written by foreigners who undoubtedly learned English via correspondence course. All these new abbreviations to deal with. Let's see now, OGM (Out Going Message), ICM (In Coming Message). Hold this button down while talking, but make sure your announcement isn't too long and that it ends before the red light goes on. All my years of engineering school hadn't quite prepared me for this instruction manual. How could it be that the dizzy little blond down the hall figured out her answering machine?

And why all these hang-ups? Sometimes, if I was lucky, I'd get a grunt. I actually learned to distinguish grunts. It's amazing, but people with different accents have distinguishable grunts.

"Hi, Dad, how are you?"

"Fine, son, but how come you never return my calls?"

"Dad, you called me?"

"Yes, four times this week."

Now I'm worried. Maybe I got my ICM confused with my OGM and my machine isn't working correctly.

"Dad, you left me four messages this week?"

"No."

"Did you leave me any messages?"

"No, I didn't."

"You called me four times and you didn't leave me a single message? Why not?"

"I don't like to speak to your machine."

"Why is that, Dad?"

"Because it's an English-speaking machine."

"Trust me, Dad, it understands Yiddish!"

For the longest time my father wouldn't leave messages, but I learned to recognize the grunt he made before he hung up.

Other people must be having problems with hang-ups too. Controlling hang-ups must be a whole science. I heard outgoing messages created with full orchestral backup. Competition was tough. I had to create a more interesting announcement tape.

This voice is not of Elliot
  it's that of his machine
Invention quite superior
  the voice is crisp and clean.

It forwards any message
  no matter short or long
But best of all its features is
  that nothing can go wrong
    - can go wrong
      - can go wrong
        - can go wrong.

That message didn't pull enough responses. Maybe it failed to inspire confidence. I had to try again.

It's Elliot
  and his machine
Which takes your message
  crisp and clean.

The beeper forwards
  all to me
Just think how happy
  you will be.

At the sound of beep
>please talk, it's fine;

Why hang up now?
>you've spent your dime.

This one worked too well. People called many times just to hear it. They also hung up many times.

Like other single people, I became aware that the telephone coupled with a telephone answering machine becomes a lifeline to the outside world. In a relatively short time, I had had to adapt to the world as it now existed for me. Then again, I could also try to modify the world to suit me a little better.

I didn't always agree with how things were done. I thought call forwarding was great, except for a few problems. To use call forwarding, you have to know where you're going before you leave your home. While you are in transit, someone is already receiving your calls. After using it, you have to return home to terminate it. What good is that? What if you want to go to Bloomingdale's before returning home?

Now I had a project. I set about redesigning call forwarding. What the world needed was Call Follow You - the ability to reprogram call forwarding from anywhere in the world, not just from your home phone. I got very involved in this project with a partner, and ultimately received a patent for Remote Call Forwarding. This project started simply because, as a single, I had a problem to solve for myself, and it resulted in a new product on the market.

I also felt that those Automated Teller Machines (ATMs) at banks were poorly designed. Anyone who's ever used one knows they're designed all wrong. Go into any bank on a Sunday morning. You'll see a line of people backed up at the money machine, because by Sunday everyone is a little short of cash. Do you know why the line is moving so slowly?

After you insert your card, WAIT, the machine wants to know if you prefer to make your transaction in English or Chinese. I have yet to run into a horde of Chinese-speaking people in my neighborhood.

After that, WAIT, the machine inquires as to which kind of transaction you wish to conduct. It's Sunday morning, you're standing there in your jogging suit. Who knows, maybe you're in the mood to transfer money from your ready credit to your checking plus. And that's the way it goes. Then it wants to know whether to get the money from your checking account, or to convert some of your pesos from your foreign currency account.

I had a much simpler solution, recognizing that most people go to the cash machine because they want cash. If I had designed the machine it would have worked very differently. Let's name it the WHEN machine. This machine calls for a slot for the bank card, and a WHEN button. Nothing else required, no instructions, not even a screen. The customer would insert his card, whereupon the machine would immediately start rolling out ten-dollar bills. $10, $20, $30... until the customer said WHEN by hitting the WHEN button. –

I had time on my hands. I used some of the time to create things of substance. I used some of the time to create things only in my head.

Pervert
(1982 - age 42)

My divorce and my move to Manhattan created a great deal of confusion, not only for me but for most of the people around me. They thought my marriage was a happy one. I knew I had to get divorced, but I could not deal with the event. I became very withdrawn and did not share the details with friends or relatives. I had the means to stop working. I sank into myself. Friends and relatives could not understand me. I couldn't understand me, either. My world had been shattered. Life became meaningless. In this new life, I didn't work too much. I walked a lot, talked to strangers, saw movies, and played with my inventions.

After a year or so of this, I decided I had to get some kind of job. Anything. I needed a reason to wake up in the morning. I mailed my resume to New York University and landed an interview.

I left my Sutton Place apartment to stroll down to Forty-second Street and Fifth Avenue for the interview. I had gotten less than two blocks from my apartment when a man slipped a piece of paper into my hand. I looked at it while I walked. It was a promotion for a parlor of some kind, where one could receive a massage and other forms of gratification. I had barely finished reading that promotion when another man slipped another paper into my hand. I examined that flyer. This place too offered erotic massages. Looking at the addresses I discovered that they were both on the same block, within two blocks of my residence. This surprised me. I thought my neighborhood was residential, and didn't suspect that such activities were going on right here. I kept walking and another man handed me a similar solicitation, containing suggestive pictures as well.

My goodness, how many of these places were there? I became more alert. Where were these flyers coming from? Now I saw the seedy characters in the doorways, looking for prospects. As I walked along, I looked back at them expectantly. My stare said, "Yes, I want one, I am a candidate." They would head right over and hand me a flyer. That sort of place was the last place on earth I would patronize but I was curious about how many of these places existed in my own neighborhood. I also wondered how many of these solicitations I would be handed between Fifty-fourth and Forty-second streets. As it turned out, I was holding over a dozen of them.

Arriving at my interview, I hastily hid these advertisements in my overcoat pocket. The interview lasted two hours (and did result in a teaching job at New York University). After I left, I headed for Fifth Avenue, still thinking about the interview. In my distraction, I walked right into the moving traffic. There was a great screech. A taxi cab came to a halt only inches away from me. The cabby was yelling at me.

As I came out of my daze, my first thought was relief that I was still alive. Then I put my hands into my pockets and felt those solicitations. A new thought occurred to me. What if I had been killed? My belongings would be sent to my family. My family would see my winter coat, full of these seedy solicitations, and conclude that that was why I had gotten divorced and had moved to Manhattan. That I had become a total pervert!

The thought made me shudder and laugh at the same time. Even those of my relatives who still didn't know English too well would understand these explicit solicitations. How would that look? I ran to the nearest trash can.

Control
(1982 - age 42)

A ll this preoccupation with appearances! Maybe I'm masking some other problem I should be dealing with. What about the fear of losing control?

In the back of my mind I always have the fear of losing it, I mean losing everything - my degrees, my home, yes, even my penis. Maybe it's not so much a fear of losing everything as it is the fear of being thrown back to a time when I had no control over anything. Yes, I guess that would be sort of like losing my penis. I suppose it's more or less all the same to me.

Why should I have a problem surrounding control? Perhaps because my life went through such a catharsis when I finally managed to take control of it. My self-discipline and self-reliance brought me to where I am today (wherever that is). I succeeded only when I took total charge of things. I have the illusion that I can do anything better by doing it, rather than trusting someone else to do it for me. When I fly, I sit up front, near the pilot's compartment. Deep down inside, I feel that if the pilot ran into trouble, I'd be the natural one to take over the controls. Mind you, I can't fly. Still, I feel as though I'd be the best one to improvise if need be. I feel like I'm some kind of chameleon, but instead of just changing colors, I change my persona completely. Sure, I'll just take over the plane, speak into the microphone in an improvised pilot's accent, hold the flight manual in one hand, and bring the plane down safely. Surely I wouldn't trust anyone else on the plane to do that.

While we're on the subject of control... Recently a girl that I had been dating for a few months revealed that she was getting an IUD. She was nervous about it. On the day she went to her gynecologist, I stayed home waiting for her and wrote this:

Oh Jennifer
  I see you dared
And now you've come here
  all prepared;

With something very
    new inside
I see you wear it
    with such pride;

But please beware
    you may not know
Mechanicals are
    quite my show;

And I have wired
    this device
To count all men
    committing vice;

And telegraph
    this count to me
Think how embarrassed
    you would be;

It's best you wear it
    just for show
But do not use it
    I will know.

Seems I had the illusion that I was going to stand guard over her jewels. That relationship didn't last long. I told her that even though I cared for her, I could never marry her because I would never marry again. It was soon after my divorce, and that's what I truly felt then. Well, her mama raised no fool and she promptly left me!

Why was I that honest? I was taught to tell the truth, and those were my true feelings at that time. It's the story of my life. I told the truth as a child, and my father almost got executed. I tell the truth as an adult, and get slapped again. I can't seem to learn.

Control, control... Take this operation. You think I'm happy about letting a doctor perform this operation? Sure, doctors go to medical school. But maybe my doctor had the lowest ranking in his class. I don't know for sure if he's competent. Or, better yet, maybe he didn't finish high school, like me! I know I'm competent. I'd probably try to perform this surgery myself if only I could reach around to that part of my body.

"Ouch, God, please don't let the doctor hurt me."

"God? Did you say God? I thought you were an agnostic."

"I am, most of the time. But not when I'm being operated on. Right now I need to believe there is a God. And like everyone else in this position, I need to feel that I can influence him, or cut a deal with him."

"Cut a deal with God?"

"Isn't that what it's all about? When people pray, aren't they trying to gain favor?"

"Elliot, you said 'Cut a deal.'"

"That's right, cut a deal. Do you ever listen to some of the things that people say? I'll tell you what I think they really mean, and you tell me they're not trying to cut a deal."

Please God, I really need that!

This is the lowest form of appeal. Just plain begging.

Why me, God?

This is an appeal to the sense of philosophy and the sense of fairness. (Pick on someone else for a change - haven't you picked on me enough?)

Jesus - I've had it!

This is a mild threat. This approach is not well thought out, because it is not quite clear how you will follow through, but it does serve to put God on notice that you won't put up with it much longer.

God loves me - He wouldn't do that to me.

This is not bad, it tries to make God feel guilty. (If it turns out that God is Jewish, or had a Jewish mother, this might prove most effective of all.)

God, if you could just do this one thing for me.

This is clearly a proposition for a deal. Presumably the deal is this: God does this one thing for you, in exchange for which you promise to get off his back.

O God, if I win the lottery I would donate one half of it to the church immediately.

This is an offer for partnership (we're in this together). In exchange for influencing the lottery, God is offered half of the take.

God, if I win the lottery, I'll donate $18 to the synagogue.

This is an attempt by Jewish people to cut a deal. It relies heavily on the popular notion that God has a special thing about the number 18.

God, I donated $18 to the synagogue this morning, Now I'm betting on the number 18181818.

This variation on the above plays on the fact that the donation was already made. (Money talks - BS walks.) It has the further advantage of communicating the desired number. This gives God simple instructions so he can't mess up. This is the same kind of person that's trying to find out God's FAX number.

The disadvantage of this last method is that if the number 18 or some variation of it does come in, the winnings would be severely diluted by the fact that four million people in Brooklyn play that number on any given day."

"You might have a case there. But Elliot, you tell me you're not religious and yet you pray. Why?"

"I'm still not perfect, but I'm working on it."

"Sure you're perfect, Elliot. You know it all, you can do it all. You don't need God, you don't need me. You could even perform this surgery on yourself if only you had longer hands, right?

"Ouch."

"Hold still"

"Ouch, ouch. Please be gentle, doctor, I'm only kidding, I couldn't perform this surgery on myself, for that I need a fine doctor like you. Ouch. Please, doctor, tell me, is it finished yet? Is there more pain?"

"Elliot, pain is how you know you are still alive! Unless you're so clever that you've figured out something else. Have you, Elliot? Have you figured it out? Let me ask you this, have you figured out anything? Have you figured out life? Have you figured out what it's all about?"

Life

No, I haven't figured out what it's all about. I have learned a little about life and a little about myself. What I have learned about myself is that I need exhilaration, excitement, constant stimulation, constant adventure. My youth offered me a variety of experiences, and I still have a great need to try new things. I started life on a train, more or less, and I still can't seem to get off it.

Starting life on a train shapes you, even if you can get off it. If you must be clever or self-reliant to survive, you become so. The urge to survive is strong. Each of us adopts techniques for it. Those techniques may outlive their usefulness, but they remain with us, because that's what we know. They are ingrained in us, staying with us even after we no longer need them. In my case I had to learn to adapt, to improvise. I learned to contract or grow as the situation required, adjusting myself like the squeeze box that I played as a child.

"Elliot, do you feel this made you different from other people?"

"I don't know that it made me different, but I think it's safe to say that I see things through differently colored glasses. My experiences are responsible for the way I look at everything. God, man, machine."

"Isn't it a burden for you to see things the way you do? Don't you resent it? Don't you wish you had a more normal childhood, a childhood without deprivation?"

"Doctor, you mean the deprivation of having to spend my youth in Russia and in a DP camp? The deprivation of having to live and experience different countries, cultures and languages? You must mean the experience of having no television, and no toys. That deprivation, right? You're asking if I missed the privilege of being raised in a middle class suburb, if I missed the joy of spending my youth at Friendly's or the local mall? Missed having gadgets and toys already imagined and created for me, so that I would not need to develop my own imagination or creativity? If I missed having television as my prime model for life? Missed commercials that fabricate needs, to fill in the emptiness that results when one has no real basic needs? What deprivation?

"I'm grateful for having been spared a privileged upbringing. Yes, things were bad, good, safe, risky, painful, funny, ugly and wonderful. But all of us, young and old, lived life. Interesting lives. As for the difficulties in adjusting in school? So it was difficult, it strengthened me. The pain? It made me appreciate the good and laugh at the silly and absurd. The easy life, or the good life - don't pray for it, because you just might get it, and it robs you. The way I see it, all you really need in life is love, a squeeze box and a little good fortune to find the right note. What about you, doctor? What do you think?"

"What do I think about what, Elliot?"

"Life, what do you think about life?"

"Sorry, Elliot, I don't have time to think. I only get paid for procedures and thinking is not a procedure, so it doesn't pay to think."

"Then please just tell me, is there going to be more pain with this procedure that you're performing?"

"Elliot, I'm not a clairvoyant."

"Please, just tell me - is there more pain? More pain? More pain? More pain? "

"Elliot, Elliot, snap out of it. You're done, you can leave. Oh, before you go, you've got us curious now. Why did you get circumcised at the age of seven? Would you tell us about that?"

"Again? I just did, doctor! I just told you the story of my whole life!"

"No, Elliot. You asked me for a pen and paper, but I told you it wasn't sterile and I couldn't let you write while we're performing surgery."

"Don't you remember, doctor? After that you asked me what my life was like."

"No, I don't think so."

"Yes, I told you what my life was like, and you told me what kind of life that was, remember?"

"Not quite, Elliot. You didn't tell us much. You started to tell us your circumcision story, and then you tuned out for a while. Please finish the story, it sounded interesting.

"No, Doc, I'm not telling it again. I've told it to too many people too many times."

"Have you thought of writing a book about it, Elliot?"

"Sure I have. I'd love to write a book. Maybe it will be made into a movie."

"What's holding you back, then?"

"Actually, the cover, doctor."

"How's that, Elliot?"

"You see, people are attracted to a book by its cover."

"So?"

"Well, there is no workable cover for my book."

"What do you mean, Elliot?"

"Look, if you write a cookbook, you put a tasty dish on the cover. If you write an auto repair manual, you put a car on the cover. So, my dear doctor, if I do write a book that features a story about my circumcision, what do you suggest I put on the cover?"

~ End ~

Dear reader,

If you enjoyed reading the book as much as I enjoyed writing it, please consider sharing it with your friends or posting a review.

Thanks
Elliot

16245120R00160

Made in the USA
Charleston, SC
11 December 2012